Andy Martin l[illegible] French at Cambridge University and writes on sports and other aspects of culture for *The Times*. He is the author of *Walking on Water* and two works of literary criticism, *The Knowledge of Ignorance* and *The Mask of the Prophet: The Extraordinary Fictions of Jules Verne*.

ALSO BY ANDY MARTIN

The Knowledge of Ignorance
The Mask of the Prophet:
the Extraordinary Fictions of Jules Verne
Walking on Water

Coming Down the Mountain

ANDY MARTIN

PHŒNIX

A PHOENIX PAPERBACK

First published in Great Britain by John Murray
(Publishers) Ltd in 1993
This paperback edition published in 1993 by Phoenix,
a division of Orion Books Ltd,
Orion House, 5 Upper St Martin's Lane,
London WC2H 9EA

The author and publishers would like to thank Glidrose Publications and Jonathan Cape Ltd for permission to reproduce an extract from *On Her Majesty's Secret Service* by Ian Fleming © Glidrose Productions Ltd 1963.

A CIP catalogue record for this book is available from the British Library

ISBN: 1 85799 074 9

Printed and bound in Great Britain by
The Guernsey Press Co. Ltd, Guernsey, Channel Islands

For the boy

And this prime matter is found in a mountain containing an immense collection of created things. In this mountain is every sort of knowledge that is found in the world. There does not exist knowledge or understanding or dream or thought or sagacity or opinion or deliberation or wisdom or philosophy or geometry or government or power or courage or excellence or contentment or patience or discipline or beauty or ingenuity or journeying or orthodoxy or guidance or precision or growth or command or dominion or kingdom or vizierate or rule of a councillor or commerce that is not present there. And there does not exist hatred or malevolence or fraud or villainy or deceit or tyranny or oppression or perverseness or ignorance or stupidity or baseness or violence or cheerfulness or song or sport or flute or lyre or marriage or jesting or weapons or wars or blood or killing that is not present there.

Abu'l-Qasim, *The Book of Knowledge*

1

In a cave on an island to the north of Norway are some rock carvings estimated to be four and a half thousand years old. One of them depicts a stylized figure whose feet merge into very long shoes curled up at the nose like Turkish slippers. His rabbit-like ears are perhaps the horns or wings of a helmet. He is pointing downhill, leaning forward into the wind. His back is straight and his knees are bent over his toes. He is carrying a hooked instrument that might be a pole or a weapon. He is presumed to be a hunter but what he is hunting is not known.

Similar carvings, dating from around 1000 BC, have been found in north-west Russia close to the White Sea. The most striking of them shows three naked men in profile also sporting elongated footgear. They are so plainly naked that they are usually known as the 'three phallic figures on skis'. Winter temperatures in these parts can drop to as low as minus 40 degrees Centigrade.

It is unlikely that these Stone Age murals are early exercises in art for art's sake. Some say that we make pictures on a wall as a form of sympathetic magic, hoping to summon up the thing represented; others that they have an educative, mythic, or allegorical function. According to one theory, they appear only in times of crisis, when the very existence of the subject is in jeopardy.

2

THE main road north out of Glasgow was blocked, so we veered west and drove up the coast through a blizzard. The dim, phosphorescent forms of Black Mount and Ben Nevis flared up out of the darkness and fled by like ghosts in the night. It wasn't the kind of west coast Callahan was used to. 'Where are the palm trees?' he complained. 'Where are the *girls*?'

I had left him almost a year before in his blue-striped baggy shorts, T-shirt, and white Foreign Legion hat. He had his face screwed into a yard-long telefoto lens. He was like that so often the lens seemed to grow straight out of his head, like the horn of a unicorn or Pinocchio's nose. In winter, Callahan and Hawaii were inseparable, like a devoted couple on a prolonged honeymoon. So when he rang from Heathrow in December 1990 he spoke as bitterly as if his wife had run off with another man.

'Finn wanted some winter shots from Europe. Told me to get my ass up to Thurso, somewhere around the Arctic Circle. You know the place?'

Ten years before a shadowy, unshaven photograph of him had been used in a publicity campaign by a bank in Holland to represent 'the kind of customer most banks wouldn't do business with'. It was inevitable that he should have become a photographer for *Surfing* magazine.

His Scottish picture featured a surfer in a red wetsuit,

with blue boots and white hat and gloves, perched on a hump-backed wall of water – and, in the background, the snow-capped Orkney mountains lit by an unearthly glow. Elfin Saffer came from California. 'This is my tropical paradise,' he said, as an icy wind whipped about our ankles and froze our faces into scowls. Saffer and Callahan both had white, white hair, bleached by sun and salt. It was like looking at two saints with haloes.

It was a week later and I was back in Cambridge putting together a lecture on the relationship between art and photography in the nineteenth century, when Simon O'Hagan called and asked me to cover the Première Neige in Val d'Isère for the *Independent on Sunday*. It was an emergency – the inaugural downhill of the skiing season was only three days away, with a providential early fall already in place, and their specialist skiing correspondent was laid up with his leg in plaster. I talked Simon into sending Callahan too.

'If you can shoot surf you can shoot snow. It's all water, isn't it?'

'Jesus, I can't even ski,' Callahan said.

'Bring your 1000 mm lens,' I said. 'You won't have to leave the hotel.'

Nobody skied on Oahu. There was a mountain there all right, or rather a volcano, but there was nothing on top but palm trees and astronomical observatories. Callahan was a natural surfer, as supple as a seal in the water. 'You know what I like about surfing with you?' he said one day. 'When I surf with the pros I feel like a kook. I love to go out with a real kook for a change, so I'm the pro.'

This time it would be different. He was the kook and I was the pro. But there was a hitch: I was rusty, very rusty. There had been no snow for a decade and I was too busy surfing anyway. Waiting for the plane to Geneva, I felt like Bob Hope in *Paleface*, a barber who has let himself in for a shootout with a gunslinger and is trying desperately to remember what he is supposed to do as he strides up the main street to his doom. 'The wind's in the east, so lean to the west. He draws from the right, so aim for your left.' Or was it the other way round? Bob Hope's skin was saved by Jane Russell, who as well as being shaped like an egg-timer turned out to be an undercover agent who could put a bullet through a fly at sixty paces. Callahan was checking his equipment and making notes on his Psion Organizer when I told him I was just going to make a quick call home.

Cosimo was a far cry from Jane Russell. He was an Alpine guide based in Cambridge and an eternal student researching a PhD in criminology. He had devoted years to a high-minded study of lowlife villains and knew more about the underworld than Dante. Already his thesis topped a thousand pages, and still the end was not in sight. He was Italian, but an Italian of the north, serious, reserved, ironic, discreet, remorselessly rational, obsessive, unforgiving. His black hair was cut short on his head, but when he took his shirt off it was like a Sikh removing his turban and his thin legs were as thickly cushioned as pylons on the piste.

Cosimo had never learned to ski, with him it was all instinct. The first time we went skiing together – in Courmayeur on the Italian side of Mont Blanc – he took me straight up to the top of the mountain, bypassing the nursery slopes. Europe was laid out like a three-dimensional map at our feet: on one side Italy, on the other France, and beyond Switzerland, with forests and lakes precisely marked out in contrasting inks, and the streamers of human habitation, railways and rivers twisting along the valleys between crenellated contours. It was like looking down on Earth from the Moon.

The sensation of omniscience passed when I considered the question of descent from the pinnacle. I was as weak as a baby; I had no idea how to walk, let alone ski. I couldn't feel my toes any more. I didn't have any toes, my legs ended in a pair of concrete boots, and I couldn't see, the map had dissolved into mist. I had frost in my hair and iced-up ears. I was nearly thirty and having second thoughts about trying to live out childhood dreams. I begged Cosimo for guidance.

'Follow me,' he said, and hissed away, economical, weightless, barely skimming the snow, swaying into turns which were more like subtle bends in an invisible stream than discrete actions with beginnings and ends.

His teaching method was drastic and punitive but it worked. I came down because there was no other way to go and breezed through the colours, green, blue, red, black. While I swerved round with the arc of the piste, he would cut away from the beaten snow and dance through the trees. He was as comfortable among cliffs and ridges and rocks as a fakir on a bed of nails. He was a Captain Cook of the mountains, always drawing up novel cartographies and searching earnestly for the North-West passage.

Cosimo was an adept of ski mountaineering, which was less a sport than a form of military strategy. He organized marathon treks through the fresh snow like Napoleon walking back from Moscow. One spring he had me sweating behind him up the Gran Paradiso, sinking up to my knees while he padded over the surface like a cat on a tiled roof. He could even ski uphill, with sealskins on the underside of his skis. We stayed the night on the Haute Route in a spartan *rifugio*, all cold water and snoring dormitories, a Nissen hut that used to be a barracks for the army. Even at 5 am, with the air like a razor and the mountains still hooded in darkness, it was good to get out again. Cosimo insisted that the dawn that is earned by toiling beneath the frosty stars was more beautiful than that watched in comfort from a bedroom window. The aesthetic was indistinguishable, in his eyes, from the ascetic.

'The partisans were great skiers,' he said, poring over a map as the eastern sky caught fire. 'You have to know the snow.' When I asked Cosimo to tell me about the secrets of snow he said it was a subject to be learned through experience alone, not in the pages of books nor from the mouths of men.

He was only happy when there were no paths and we had to make our own. He recalled the time one man sailed off the side of the mountain at Courmayeur and died; two men were following in his tracks, like drivers in the fog fixated on the taillights in front, and they died too. During the war an Italian guide was coerced by the Germans into leading them against his own people. He lit the way with a torch to the edge of a precipice and skied resolutely into thin air; the enemy, lured on by his light, tumbled to their doom.

But all that was long ago. Cambridge was like Plato's cave and for years I had been watching flickering shadows on the wall. I needed Cosimo, he alone had the knowledge. All I got was his answerphone.

'Looks like you're on your own, Andy,' said Callahan over my shoulder.

3

I CALLED from Geneva and I called from Val d'Isère. Still no Cosimo.

But nine thousand feet up the Rocher de Bellevarde, beneath a blue immensity, by some obscure miracle, I had my old skills returned to me more or less intact, just a little dusty for being stashed away for so long. Once I was back in ski boots and locked into my skis it was as if I'd never been out of them. The air was clean and cold and blew away the fog in my brain. My mounting anxiety on the spiralling drive from Geneva, my finalist's butterflies as we straightened out into town past the frozen lakes, my quiet desperation in the cable-car going up to the slopes, had all been unnecessary. The freshly fallen snow glittered like sequins as I picked out some gentle flowing lines at the top of the mountain, knitting together my turns without a hitch, my skis throwing up spumes of powder like confetti. Planting the poles, weighting and unweighting, bending and straightening: it was all there. It was a cinch. I still had the rhythm.

Callahan eyed me from the crest of the slope with grudging admiration. It couldn't be easy being the learner for a change. I had given him enough to get started, the bare basics: snowplough, pole, turn, snowplough, pole, turn. His skis formed a closed V. He opened them a crack and began to slide cautiously down the mountain. He had a good stance for a beginner: tight and straight and, above all, vertical. It was going into his first turn that things started to fall apart. His skis stuttered and his feet splayed out wide and his arms went up over his head. Instead of a V he was now an X. He was wobbling and gyrating and rotating his poles like propellers. He wheeled around on one ski and bombed towards me, limbs threshing the air.

'Snowplough, snowplough!' I yelled as I dived for cover.

My nose and ears were jammed full of snow and my legs were twisted like the strands of a rope. I shook my head and wiped my Raybans and looked up expecting to see Callahan wrapped round a fir tree, or upside down in a drift. Instead he was standing just a couple of yards away, elbows propped on his poles, grinning down at me.

'Come on, Andy, get off your ass and let's shred.' With that he span round, went into a racing crouch and shot down the piste in an unswerving straight line, whooping like a redskin. He dipped and rose, then dropped out of sight.

I didn't catch up with him till the bottom. He was leaning against a fence, with his face raised to the giant sun like a man in a trance, a Diet Coke in one hand.

'To think we're being paid for this,' he said, without opening his eyes.

'I thought', I panted, 'you said you didn't ski.'

'I guess those tips of yours must have done the trick.' He gave me a look of unimpeachable innocence and then returned his gaze to inward meditation. 'Of course, it might have been something I picked up back in California – the only place in the world where you can surf in the morning and ski in the afternoon. Funny how these things come back to you.'

4

IN the beginning Moses came down the mountain but there was no snow and there were no skis. Next, there was snow, but there were no skis. Then, in the fullness of time, there was snow *and* there were skis. It was the Golden Age. But suddenly, out of a clear blue sky, there were skis – *but there was no snow.* The Greenhouse Effect had struck with a vengeance. Now a new age was dawning – the Return of Snow. The bare peaks of the Alps, as shocking and unexpected as Santa Claus stripped of his whiskers, were once again as thickly covered as a Christmas pudding smothered with whipped cream.

For the last few years, the Critérium International de la Première Neige, held at the beginning of December, had had to be called off since the *première neige* hadn't actually fallen until January. But this year conditions in Val d'Isère were perfect. Even the concrete polygons housing discos and cinemas and souvenir shops, as alien as flying saucers among the classic A-frame timber chalets and medieval church of the old Haute Savoie village, were harmonized and redeemed beneath their thick coat of brilliant white.

The Première Neige was the opening event of the men's World Cup, the Grand Prix circuit that took skiers on a winter-long rollercoaster ride through Europe, Asia and the Americas. But the Première Neige was more than that, it was a ritual celebration of the Fall, a recollection of that original snow that came upon the earth like grace some 2800 million years ago when the planet cooled and the oceans formed and continents rammed into one another like dodgem cars and the high places were divided from the steamy lowlands. We were paying homage to the frozen water that transformed mountains into slippery slopes and made the world fit to ski.

The earliest known ski, discovered in Sweden, has been pollen-dated to as far back as 2500 BC. The Stone Age skier could choose between two short broad skis (popular in Asia), two long thin ones (the Nordic type), or one long and one short (one for gliding the other for pushing). Norsemen were buried with their skis on, like pharaohs with their servants, to assist in the journey to Valhalla. It was for love of skiing that the goddess Skadi deserted her husband Njord and the coast to return to the sacred mountain. In the Finnish saga of the *Kalewala*, the legendary hero Lemminkainen – celebrated in a tone poem by Sibelius – has a ski stick that causes the snow to smoke. *Mu-ma*, or 'wooden horses', as the primitive skis of the Mongols were known to the Chinese, may have given rise to the legend of *hippopodes*, men with horses' hoofs, recorded by Pliny the Elder in Book IV of the *Historia naturalis*.

Soldiers, trappers, miners, merchants, postmen, all had skied in the pursuit of objectives to which skiing was incidental. In the Nordic countries skiing was a test of skill and courage and an initiation into adulthood. But it was not until the second half of the nineteenth century in the Alps, and in Scandinavian expatriate enclaves in the Rockies, Australia, New Zealand, and

South America, that skiing began to be perceived as an end in itself, like poetry.

In 1888 Norwegian zoologist and explorer Fridtjof Nansen undertook an epic journey on skis, crossing Greenland from east to west in forty days and not washing for a month. His subsequent book, *Paå Ski Over Grönland*, swiftly translated into English and German, established him as the Rousseau of the North, exalting Nature and the noble savages who lived on seal blubber and went naked in their igloos, and revelling in the romance of skiing:

> Can there be anything more beautiful than the northern winter landscape, when the snow lies foot-deep, spread as a soft white mantle over field and wood and hill? Where will you find more freedom and excitement than when gliding swiftly down the hillsides through woods, your cheeks brushed by the sharp cold air and frosted pine branches – with eye, brain and muscles alert and prepared to meet every unknown obstacle and danger which the next instant may throw in your path? Civilization is, as it were, washed clean from the mind and left far behind with the city atmosphere and city life; your whole being is wrapped in your ski and the surrounding nature.

In a year's time Val d'Isère would be the site of the Olympic Downhill. Even in December 1990 most of the racers were already preparing themselves mentally for February 1992. The World Cup was returning later in the season to test out the new course created specifically for the Games, the east-facing 'Face de Bellevarde'.

But the Première Neige remained loyal to the long-established descent on the west side of the mountain.

The aptly named 'OK' course had a great foaming blonde head on it, which had been groomed, trimmed and tonsured, and finally sprayed with water to create a slick, glassy finish. The names of its two creators, Henry Oreiller and Jean-Claude Killy – whence the acronym – evoked something of its ambiguity, its intimidating seductiveness: it was a white pillow (*oreiller*), plump and fluffy, lulling you into restful oblivion; and it was murderous.

The downhill is the exact opposite of deep-sea divers coming up too fast from the ocean floor and just as dangerous a habit. Dangling a couple of hundred feet above the earth in a chairlift, I peered down on the orange netting that ribboned around the mountain and marked out the limits of the course. The OK was around three kilometres long and one kilometre down: a 1:3 drop. Even on 1:12 roads the signs warn you to stay in low gear. Here the whole point was to go straight into top and forget your brakes. Turn only if you have to.

There was an old man in the chairlift with me. His name was Pierre Penser (at least that's the way it sounded). He reminded me of the High Lama of Shangri-La in James Hilton's *Lost Horizon* who had known Napoleon and could choose when to die. He told me he was sixty-seven years old but I would as easily have believed 167, though his deeply tanned face was as smooth as polished oak. The mountains were his backyard and when he skied it was as if he had wings on. But even he blew out his cheeks and expelled a puff of admiration at the twisting track below. 'For the *descente*,' he said, 'it is necessary to be a little *casse-cou*' (literally 'breakneck').

The race was on Saturday morning. I was due to file two thousand words to come out on Sunday and it was already Friday. The last training session was underway so I hung around at the finish while Callahan scouted out locations up at the start. He was looking for 'the one picture that says it all'.

The Première Neige was the opening skirmish in a long campaign to come. Now, before the hostilities commenced in earnest, there was an opportunity for veterans to show off their scars and medals and for young bloods to look heedlessly forward to their inevitable triumphs to come.

Pirmin Zurbriggen was escorting Sergio Tacchini clients about the slopes. Having paid several million dollars to have his name emblazoned on every banner and marquee and official sheet of paper, not to mention the race bibs that turned skiers into extremely fast advertising hoardings, the Italian sportswear manufacturer (taking over from Café Lavazza) was the chief benefactor of the World Cup. Zurbriggen had been one of its chief beneficiaries. Now, at the age of twenty-eight, the idol of Swiss ski racing, having won everything there was to win, World Cups and Olympics, downhill and slalom, he had retired, unwrinkled, to give everyone else a chance. Zurbriggen had curly blond hair and blue eyes and an angelic wife and child. He was taking a degree in catering and management and following his father into the hotel business.

But he was a frustrating presence for this year's skiers: at Mount Hutt in August, volunteering as one of the out-of-contest 'forerunners' – who clear the course and test the timing mechanisms – he clocked a better time than the official winner. 'It would have been faster if only I hadn't been out of training,' he apologized. A devout Catholic, Zurbriggen had made numerous pilgrimages to Lourdes, but he didn't really need to. His fortune was estimated at fifteen million Swiss francs.

Now he was a spectator and there was a vacuum at the top that someone had to fill. As the main contenders – Swiss, Austrians, Norwegians – swooped into the press area, trailing clouds of glory, they were set upon by packs of snarling newshounds. One man stood alone and unsought after. He pushed up his goggles and pulled off his helmet and sighed like a kamikaze pilot who has just missed his shot at eternity. Tsuyoshi Tomii's English was bad and my Japanese was worse.

I pointed to the printout of training times for the previous day. T. Tomii was somewhere near the bottom of the list.

'Yesterday?' I said.

'Bad,' he said. Then he pointed at his right leg. 'Leg,' he said. 'Bad.'

'Today?' I said, gesturing at the mountain behind him.

'Good.'

'Tomorrow?'

'Very good.'

'Sayonara,' I said, bidding him farewell.

I suspected that Tsuyoshi was holding something back, but what I didn't realize was that with small variations his story would be repeated by most of the other skiers that I spoke to: yesterday, bad; today, good; tomorrow, very good. It was a novel in a nutshell, an entire philosophy condensed to a pea.

5

RUMOUR had it that one man was carrying his leg around in a jar. Then it narrowed down to just a spare ligament, surplus to requirements. The man it belonged to was Martin Bell.

Callahan and I went to see him in the ziggurat where the British team was staying, right opposite the contest course. They started ahead of the field: all they had to do was walk across the road and catch a lift up the mountain. It was only after that that they fell behind. The British are at a disadvantage where skiing is concerned. We are a lowland country, with not enough snow and no serious mountains, hopelessly dominated by Alpine nations and Americans. It is ironic then that we should have invented the game.

Today 'downhill skiing' seems almost a tautology, like 'unmarried bachelor'. But it was not always thus. At the beginning of the twentieth century Norwegian traditionalists, content to dawdle along the valley, still frowned on the idea of climbing up mountains only to come flying down them again. Arnold Lunn was an English heresiarch who broke with the old orthodoxy and the Vatican of Oslo. Born in India in the same year that Nansen crossed Greenland, at the zenith of Empire, and living to see its nadir, Lunn seized on skiing as an opportunity for Britain once again to lead a civilizing mission, this time to the mountains of Europe and the world.

He was the first to elucidate the antithesis between Nordic *skilaufen* and Alpine *skifahren*, between cross-country on the one hand, suited to the gentle undulations of the Scandinavian terrain, and ski-running on the other, adapted to the cliffs and canyons of Switzerland. He divided people up into laufers and runners: if you were a laufer you went through life traversing; if you were a runner you took the plunge. He defined skiing's *sine qua non* as the 'dive downhill' and its ideal geometry as 'the straight line'. He turned it from a means of getting from A to B into a sport, an art form, a morality play. Now, as in cricket, as in football, the masters had been overtaken and humiliated by their students.

Martin Bell had been brought up in Scotland and went to school in Austria. He spoke fluent German. This gave him an edge over his compatriots and by the age of eighteen he was already Britain's number one in downhill. A lot of people thought he was the *only* one. At the Calgary Olympics in 1988 he had placed eighth. For the Austrians or the Swiss, this would have counted as a national disaster. For the British, it was a triumph.

But our best downhill skier, with our highest result ever in the discipline, was cheated of glory. He was overshadowed not just by the men who came ahead of him, but by another Englishman who came behind him. Eddie 'the Eagle' Edwards, the bespectacled plasterer turned ski-jumper, had monopolized media attention at Calgary. Martin came eighth and earned a paragraph on the back page; Eddie came last and was all over the front page. It was enough to dishearten anybody.

Eighth was Martin's best result. He was touted as Britain's Great White Hope, but after that quasi-victory he had slid down the rankings. He was twenty-six and almost a has-been. Fortunately, he had pinpointed the problem and eliminated it. That ligament. It was the cause of all his troubles – while it was still in his knee – and now it was in a jar. Callahan heard he had it put in the jar so he could show it round and say, 'There, that was what was holding me back.'

'It puts him under a lot of pressure,' said Callahan. 'What's he going to have taken out next time he loses?'

Callahan wanted to take a shot of the jar, but Bell had left it at home.

'How are all your other ligaments and stuff?' he said.

'So far so good,' said Bell.

So far he hadn't competed.

Callahan liked to sit in on interviews. He would lope around the room taking shots from odd angles and poking his lens in people's faces and every now and then chipping in a question. Other writers said they hated working with Callahan because he got in the way. They wanted a confessional atmosphere with no outside interference.

Martin Bell was tanned, taut-jawed, and short-haired. He had written a book called *Let's Go Skiing* and the flap described him as 'Britain's most successful skier ever'. It also said the book was 'lively', a sinister code-word that had probably put paid to any hopes he might have had of becoming a writer instead. Sales weren't too good and he was grateful I'd bought a copy.

It wasn't just the jar and the book that were putting pressure on Martin Bell. 'Last year was my worst year,' he admitted. As if it wasn't enough to be thrashed by every Austrian and Swiss on skis, last season his younger brother, Graham, started beating him too. Martin was the thinker of the pair, agonizingly self-critical, a martyr to skiing; Graham was the rebel and hell-raiser and hedonist who liked to jump off cliffs and get paid for it when he wasn't doing downhill. Martin anticipated retiring quietly and contemplating the river at Mortlake where he lived or buying a chalet in the Alps; Graham was an adrenalin junkie who couldn't kick the habit of going fast and was unable even to imagine doing anything else.

'Our parents were keen on walking and camping and used to take us round the Snowdon Horseshoe,' Graham said. 'I always got left behind because I was small, but I was never carried. Everyone would disappear and I would stay there on the side of the mountain completely alone at four years old. They never came back for me. They would stop and I had to catch up, then they set off again.' Twenty years later he was still trying to catch up, chasing phantoms down the mountain. Downhill began to seem like a kind of psychosis induced by infantile trauma.

Now for the first time in a decade someone not called Bell was ranked number one in the country. His name was Ronald Duncan. Martin Bell and Duncan were contemporaries. But while Martin had kept on skiing for Britain, Ronald had gone to university for three years. Now he was not only a BSc but he was skiing faster as well. There was no justice in the world and Martin had every right to feel bitter about it. But he didn't sound bitter. He said, 'It's good when you have competition from your own team. Then you're prepared.' He was ranked 73rd in the world.

Apart from a degree and a thirteenth in Sweden in 1990, Duncan had another advantage over the Bell brothers: a nickname. Everyone called him 'Boris' and made him out as an absent-minded or mad professor. He had wiry hair and a gap-toothed smile. One of his friends said of him, 'He is not of this earth.' He was from Scotland.

I had skied Scotland a few times. The Scottish mountains may not be the biggest in the world, but they're among the most arduous. On the summit of Cairngorm the wind hits Gale Force Eight almost every day. Coming down is like trying to ski in a windtunnel. When I came down the White Lady in Aviemore in the schuss position, tucked up like an egg, I was still barely travelling at 1 mph; sometimes I was going backwards. It can be so cold you think your face is going to fall off; other times the temperature rises so fast the snow recedes up the mountain faster than you can get down. I once went skiing there with a Lacanian psychoanalyst named Alf. 'What's the psychology of skiing?' I asked him. 'It's an exercise in humiliation,' he said. 'Especially in Scotland.' He counselled me to 'enjoy the pain'. Still it was a friendly place with the kind of camaraderie I imagine Christians in the Coliseum lion pit enjoyed.

Boris's parents owned a toyshop in Dundee. Boris had gone to Magdalene College in Cambridge, which was more famous for its sportsmen than its scholars. Most Magdalene men played rugby or cricket and skipped classes. Boris skied and skipped classes instead. Most Magdalene men spoke with inane upper-class English accents. Boris spoke with a Scottish accent instead. Most Magdalene men studied 'Land Economy', which was a fancy name for farming. Boris took theoretical physics. 'I couldn't spell,' he said, 'so it had to be something practical.' In his first postgraduate year Boris was ranked

350th in the world. But aerobic tests at Cambridge had convinced him he had the physical potential to overcome – 'I was among the top ten they'd ever tested in any sport.'

Boris believed it was only his equipment that was holding him back and knew he could win a World Cup race. So he had fixed up a new deal with the German manufacturers Völkl who gave him the pick of their skis. Still it was hard to make ends meet. When he wasn't on the circuit Boris lived in a bed-sit in Brixton where there wasn't room for both a bed and his skis. At night he would pull down a bed from the wall.

One year the British team was so broke the management had to take away their skis. Now they were flush with increased sponsorship and expectations. I had read in the *Evening Standard* on the plane coming over that 'the British Ski Federation is confident things will change'. Among the eager young men on the ground positive thinking was rampant. They all had good reason for optimism: they had a new coach. His name was Hans Anewanter and he was Austrian. His last job was coaching Lichtenstein.

He spoke heavily accented English in a clipped, concise manner that gave nothing away. He was sure the Brits would perform well this year. What I wanted to know was his formula for improved results. He thought about this one for a bit. I had my pen poised in anticipation. Like the British team, I felt I was on the verge of a breakthrough, all I needed was a scoop. Anewanter spoke. 'Improved results: this gives confidence.' You couldn't improve until you'd improved and then you'd improve. I wrote it down, but I didn't think I'd found the answer I was looking for.

6

THE British Alpine squad were sponsored by Drambuie, although the only sign of it was the logo on their kit: they stuck to mineral water and orange juice. The Austrians must have been sponsored by Moët et Chandon. They held a press conference where I was besieged by brimming, bubbling women thrusting cocktails and hors d'oeuvres at me. The Crêtes Blanches hotel which they had taken over had been temporarily renamed the 'Asics Information Centre'.

Asics was the name of a wealthy Japanese sportswear manufacturer that provided the Austrian team with clothes and a lot more besides. It was an acronym for *Anima sana in corpore sano*. In 1992 Asics running shoes would run the Olympic flame to Val d'Isère and Barcelona. The room was packed out with television cameras and microphones. The Director of the Winter Sports Division made a speech in Japanese (translations were available in English, French and German). The highlight of the event was the unveiling of the new Asics 'downhill suit', designed especially for the Austrian team. It shimmered like a Lycra rainbow.

Katz Funakoshi was wearing another Asics creation, the more rugged everyday skisuit lit up with polychromatic explosions. He was the European Sales Manager. He explained to me that the company philosophy was 'function first, then fashion'. Asics had set up a research laboratory in Austria and the high-tech leotards had been tested in windtunnels before being exposed to the downhill, 'the ultimate test'. The fabric was called DH Special Bonding and was slick and seamless and supple. Even the zip was stretchable.

It was almost an unfair advantage. In January 1979 the Canadian Ken Read won the downhill at Morzine, but he was disqualified for wearing a suit that was too fast. The new skintight fabrics had only recently come in and there were design flaws: they allowed no moisture out so you could drown in your own sweat; if you fell they were so smooth you'd never stop. So the Fédération Internationale de Ski (the governing body, known as FIS for short) introduced a requirement that the suit should let through a given quantity of air under a given pressure. When they pumped air into Ken Read's suit it blew up like a balloon. Karl Kahr, the Austrian coach, said that Read would have won anyway and it was a pity that rules were rules. But the next year the Austrians had new suits.

If this had been a war instead of a sporting contest, I would have backed Austria. They not only had faster clothes but more soldiers than anyone else. There were only twelve skiers, but they were backed up by serried ranks of managers, coaches, physios, and 'servicemen', whose job it was to nurse the hardware – making sixty-one in all. Some way behind them came Switzerland with forty-three men, and France and Italy with thirty-five and thirty-four respectively. The British contingent was a modest six. Not as modest as Ireland and Australia though. They came not in battalions but single spies.

The solo operators were the unsung heroes of the World Cup. The downhill course took only two minutes or so if you knew what you were doing. But months and years went into preparing for those few moments. Organization and training – and the finance that made them possible – were the keys to success. It's not so hard to win when you've got sixty sidekicks tending to your skis and cheering you on. It's a different, more epic story when you're on your own.

Ireland were staying in a creaking wooden chalet at the old end of town. They were down on the list as having two representatives. But even that was an exaggeration: one of them turned out to be in Val d'Isère to promote 'Jello-Shots', a brand of alcoholic jelly; the other was Denis O'Brien.

Every country which had its own skiing federation and was affiliated to FIS, was allowed to enter two racers. O'Brien assured me that there was an Irish Ski Federation. But who was in it?

'I am,' he said.

O'Brien's main fear was that FIS would close the loophole by bringing in qualifying races and that he wouldn't qualify. 'It's all the fault of the Senegalese guy who skied Kitzbühel last year – snowploughed all the way. Gives the smaller countries a bad name.' There was an ominous rumour that the tailenders would be cut out and the race narrowed down to the top thirty. Where was he on the computer rankings?

'I've no idea. How low does it go?'

He was the son of the captain of the Irish Rugby XV back in the fifties and he looked like he would make a fine rugby player himself, with broad shoulders and strapping arms and legs. The freckles on his boyish face and the tuft of brown hair that stuck up on the crown of his head gave him the innocence and charm of a teenage elf, but the brutal truth was that, for a downhiller, he was old, he was ancient, he was a druid. He was thirty.

To the Swiss and the Austrians, skiing was as natural as breathing, and they started as soon as they could walk; they barely even noticed that they were skiing, it was the same as being alive. For the English and the Irish it was a late discovery, like sex, and once they got the hang of it there was no stopping them. O'Brien had started as a teenager on the one artificial slope in Ireland, then graduated to Scotland. He'd been on and off the circuit for the last ten years and dreamed of representing his country at the Olympics and getting sponsored by Guinness.

He was always broke, or nearly. He reckoned it cost £22–23,000 just to get round to all the events. His winnings were nil. Officially, skiing was one of the last remaining amateur sports. O'Brien was a genuine amateur, one of the few left. The contests only paid peanuts, even if you won (£1,800 was the maximum paycheque in 1990), but some of the top skiers earned an annual six-figures in endorsements from car manufacturers and watchmakers, while others doubled up as perpetual students or customs officers, all expenses paid by their governments. O'Brien scrounged what crumbs he could from assorted ski-gear companies and moonlighted as a package-tour rep in Verbier. To add another string to his bow he was doing a course in 'remedial massage'.

'Don't you mind coming last?' That was Callahan. He must have finished a roll.

'Last year I actually beat somebody. What you've got to remember is that the competition at the bottom of the field is just as intense as at the top. There's a Belgian and a Pole skiing – I'm hoping to beat them, but if I finish I'm happy.'

O'Brien had tried his hand at speed skiing – over a straight one kilometre course of sheer ice – and had clocked up 191 km per hour. 'I'm all right on the straights. The trouble is the turns. I've got the balls. It's just my technique I worry about.'

He didn't worry about accidents and cited in support the case of the record holder in speed skiing (over 200 km per hour), five times world champion. 'Killed in a car crash the other day in Texas. I feel safe on the mountain.'

I offered O'Brien a drink. He asked for a mint tea. He was a serious racer and he was in training. This was likely to be his last season on the circuit. Even if the men from FIS didn't stop him first, he was going to run out of money anyhow. This year was his swansong.

'He's already history,' said Callahan as we went out into the night again, buttoning up our collars against the icy air.

'At least he's articulate,' I said.

'Show me the Irishman who isn't,' said Callahan.

I wanted to put my money on O'Brien as a long-shot. He would be around 1000:1. Callahan humped his lens over his shoulder and shook his head. Whether he was shaking it at me or O'Brien I don't know.

'Can you put money on the *slowest* guy?'

O'Brien had the slowest time out of sixty-seven skiers in the first training run. He was twenty-seven seconds off the lead. His name was on the bottom of every list you could find. 'I'll be quicker tomorrow,' he said and I believed him. I identified with the Irishman. I wasn't just backing him, I was flying down the mountain alongside him, I was in his boots, feeling the adrenalin rush, the vertiginous glide, the spooky weightlessness as he took off over the jumps. He wasn't representing Ireland any more, he was representing me.

When O'Brien rounded the last bend in Friday's training run and shot down the schuss, I dug Callahan in the ribs and scoffed at his lack of faith. The clock put my man some way off the leaders, but he was still a second or so ahead of the slowest.

He had a shamrock painted on the back of his helmet – it was his equivalent of carrying a torn ligament around in a jar. I know because I saw it when he was face down in the snow.

Val d'Isère had acquired a reputation among the *cognoscenti* for being relatively benign, a gentle introduction to the rigours of the season to come. Some of the skiers disdainfully referred to it as the *autobahn* and were already looking ahead to the winding goat tracks and corridors of the Hahnenkamm at Kitzbühel, where only a year before the Canadian Brian Stemmle had been ripped open in a high-speed fall. O'Brien didn't agree. 'To them it's piss-easy. To me it's still a challenge. So it's probably more fun for me than it is for them.'

The course architects were sick of hearing the OK put down and derided. So they had stiffened it up this year: a steeper start, tighter bends, more jumps, and – in the home stretch – a deeper compression: they had dug it out more so you had to come at it faster to get over it, or face landing on a slight incline. Maybe O'Brien caught the lip, because it was after that he went haywire. In his novel *Séraphita,* set in Norway, Balzac talks of skiers having 'the frightening adroitness of sleepwalkers who, oblivious to all the consequences of their mass and the dangers of the slightest deviation, can run along the edge of roofs and yet keep their balance under the influence of an unknown force.' It was as if O'Brien had been roughly awoken from a dream and had gone over the edge of the roof. He landed at an awkward angle, leaned over too much one way, then he corrected and leaned over too much the other way. First his right leg went up in the air, and then his left.

O'Brien had a secret strategy he let me in on. 'The top guys, see, they all ski the same line – the *fall line,* the fastest way from top to bottom. They go first so by the time I go there's a groove in the snow. All I have to do is stay in the groove.'

He got his balance back but he couldn't stay in the groove. He was drawing a fall line all of his own, heading for the luminous orange sheeting that marked the limit of the course and weighting like mad to get back on to the right line again.

He was perhaps only a hundred yards from the finish when he hit. He bounced, then somersaulted, leaving his skis behind, landed and span down towards the finish line, coming to a halt only a few body lengths away from the gate.

'Are you all right?' I asked, helping to excavate him from the trench he had just dug with his head.

'No, I'm not,' he said, spitting snow. 'I'm pissed. That was my fastest run yet.'

The Première Neige on Saturday was won by an Austrian, the veteran Leonhard Stock, wearing the Asics downhill suit, followed by Franz Heinzer of Switzerland and another Austrian. Boris and the Bells were down among the thirties and forties. I was on the phone correcting my story most of the night while Callahan attended an orgy at the Hotel Altitude.

7

CALLAHAN had ambitions as a writer. He had read Hemingway's *The Old Man and the Sea* and was convinced he could do something along the same lines. 'Shit, I can catch fish too.'

He had once written a piece for *Surfing* on the World Amateur Championships in Japan. 'I spent a week digging for scoops, in-between shots. Got the low-down on all the hot locals. The inside track on the top guys. Vibes, women, waves – it had it all. By the time Finn had finished with it there was nothing left but the pictures.'

When I asked Finn why he didn't let Callahan do the writing as well, he said, 'Would you ask a sprinter to run the marathon? Callahan is great over short distances. But he has no stamina. Give him a moment and he'll make an epic out of it. That's why he's good on snap-shots. But give him a real epic and all he'll give you is – moments.'

Callahan had rented a BMW with snow-chains but he never bothered to put them on. 'You want to know the worst thing you could do on a road like this?' he said, as we skidded round a bend on the way back to Geneva. 'I'll tell you – *brake*. Don't ever brake. If you brake, you'll *break*.' It was in-between hitting the back of another car, chasing a herd of goats and being stopped by the police that Callahan told me about the night before.

Callahan leaves the Altitude with an Italian girl called Gabriella and she takes him to The Office. They've hardly sat down before she says to him, straight out, 'You want an orgasm?' He can't believe his ears. For years he's been waiting for a woman to say exactly this to him and now when it finally happens it comes as a shock. He is just a Hawaiian boy and has led a sheltered life. 'It's mainly vodka with whipped cream,' Gabriella says. 'Make it a double,' says Callahan. She goes to the counter and comes back with a cocktail shaker. 'OK, lie down,' she says. Callahan lies down, stretched out on the tabletop like he's waiting for an operation. She shakes up the contents of the shaker, screws the lid off and stuffs it down the front of her jeans with the liquid foaming over the top of her belt. By this time a small but enthusiastic crowd has formed around Callahan's table and is offering advice and cheers of encouragement. She wedges a long cocktail glass between Callahan's thighs with all the exaggerated delicacy of a brain surgeon and starts to rotate her hips, like she's spinning a hoola-hoop, then buzzing like a chain-saw, and still she doesn't spill a drop. Finally she eases herself up on to the table and spreads her knees around Callahan and swoons forward with a climactic moan, tipping the white fluid into the glass. The glass is soon overflowing so she wriggles forward and empties the dregs straight into Callahan's mouth. 'Now I know what a blow-job tastes like,' he says to her as he hauls himself up.

'Do you know what she said to me next?' he said. '*Now give me one!*' He savoured the phrase. 'Those Italian women really know how to party. Too bad you missed all the action.'

We were on the plane flying back to London and

Callahan was writing a postcard to his girlfriend Jane in Hawaii. 'She's happy it's winter over here,' he said. 'She doesn't have to worry about naked European women on the beach.' He gazed pensively down on the mountains twenty thousand feet below. 'What's the next stop on the World Cup?' he said.

'Italy,' I said.

'Jesus, is that some sort of omen or what?' he said.

'How do you mean?'

'Why don't we keep going – see out the rest of the tour? We've got to make up for missing Hawaii somehow.'

But running away with the white circus wasn't as easy as it sounded. Not only were there too many events, but some were happening simultaneously. As it wound around the globe the World Cup kept the sexes puritanically apart, not just in different hotels but in different countries, so the men could be in Italy while the women were in Japan, or vice-versa.

'No problem,' Callahan said. 'Forget the women.'

When there was a slalom, a giant slalom, a super-G and a downhill all in one place, as sometimes happened, one event could last a week. Meanwhile I still had lectures to write.

'Stick to the downhill,' he said. 'It's the only thing that matters.' Slalom and even giant slalom were for wimps; super-G was only a squashed-up slowed-down downhill. There were ten downhills over the course of the season. If we could sell the stories and pictures to the *Independent on Sunday*, and to American magazines, we might just about break even. Between contests he'd go off and shoot waves and I'd go off and give classes.

The complicated itinerary of the World Cup would

take us, after France and Italy, to Germany, Austria, Switzerland, the United States and Canada. Not so much a downhill as a descent into the labyrinth.

Ernest Hemingway took up skiing in Canada after the First World War, despite the bullet wounds to his leg, and it was the prospect of the Alps as much as Paris that drew him back to Europe. In the twenties he spent most of his winters in the mountains. In his story 'Cross-Country Snow', two young men go skiing together in Switzerland and fear that their lives are changing and they'll never go skiing again: 'Don't you wish we could just bum together?' George says to Nick Adams, Hemingway's fictional counterpart. 'Take our skis and go on the train to where there was good running and then go on and put up at pubs and go right across the Oberland and up the Valais and all through the Engadine and just take repair kit and extra sweaters and pyjamas in our rucksacks and not give a damn about school or anything.'

Callahan was the same way, he wanted to keep skiing all winter and never stop.

'Come on, we'll have a great time. Ski our brains out for free.'

8

On the mantelpiece in my grandmother's house in Forest Gate was a snowdome. When you shook it, it snowed. The trees and the cottage and the sleigh beneath the glass were permanently wrapped in a duvet of white powder. Uncle Pat brought it back from Canada on one of his trips home.

'That's what it's like in Canada all the time,' he said. 'Sometimes it's so beautiful it blinds you. It's like walking on feathers.'

Uncle Pat had spiky white hair like Jack Frost and a blue serge suit and spoke with an American accent. He told me he lived near the North Pole, amid wolves and bears and reindeers and glaciers millions of years old. Whole towns regularly disappeared under the snow. Sometimes it was so cold you couldn't speak, the words froze in your throat and wouldn't come out until spring.

When I was ten Uncle Pat offered to take me back to Canada with him. We would go and prospect for gold together. The gold was under the snow, it was inside mountains, just lying there. I had heard dark rumours about Uncle Pat. He was a geologist, a gambler, a womanizer, a con man, from the hard-drinking Irish side of the family, the Hanlons. He ended up inside for fraud, but for years I hankered after following in his tracks.

Mr Morris was my first geography teacher and showed

me where Canada was on the globe. The Rockies were the backbone of America. One day Mr Morris was exploring the intricacies of cumulus and nimbus and cirrus, and cirrostratus and nimbostratus and cirrocumulus. Some clouds went with sunny days and others went with rain. Outside the sky was low and flat and milky. 'Looking at the clouds today,' Mr Morris said, pointing through the windows, 'we would predict snow.' It was at that exact moment that the first flakes of the winter began to fall: the size of mice, of doves, of lambs, they soon turned the football field white and covered up the lines. Mr Morris seemed to me not just a Welshman, but a druid, a conjuror who could pull white rabbits out of his hat, a witch-doctor with magical powers at whose behest the winds blew and the seasons changed. He taught us that every crystal was an equilateral hexagon, that in all the history of the world there had never been two exactly the same and yet they were all alike. But individual snowflakes were as fugitive as moonbeams or falling stars and melted away before your gaze.

I built my own sled out of wood, but the runners were too low and it sank like a waterlogged boat. In the end my parents bought me one made of tubular steel, painted red, with cherrywood slats across the top. My twin brother Unc and I rode it all the way from the top of Bedfords Hill down to the stream in the woods far below. One year I went to look for it and it wasn't there any more. 'I gave it to the boy next door,' my mother explained. 'I thought you'd outgrown it.'

Snow stole up on us like a fairy godmother in the night. I woke as if in a dream to find houses, trees, roads all made of ice-cream and spun sugar. What had been hills were now mountains, packed with precipices and deadly ravines. In those days winter was winter. England metamorphosed into another country far away, in which the normal laws and everyday timetable were suspended. If the weather was happily cold enough, school was cancelled. To venture beyond the front door was an expedition requiring wellington boots, a shovel, and heroic reserves of courage and stamina.

At assembly the headmaster announced that one of us would not be coming back, the victim of an avalanche in Switzerland. A winter fall was the equivalent of the Flood, wiping out those who were unprepared, purifying the old world and filling it with perils. I read a story in which an H-bomb blasted the earth further away from the sun and we all became Eskimos and lived in igloos. I prayed for that beneficent bomb to go off.

Two lumps of coal and a carrot are sitting in the middle of a field; how did they get there? That was easy – they were all that was left of a snowman in the spring. I hated the thaw and longed to go into hibernation for the summer. I knew that if you only rode fast enough you could follow the sun around the world; I wanted to chase after the vanishing snow.

9

'ALL right,' I said.

'You'll do it?'

'Yes.'

'Promise?'

'You're running away from your responsibilities as a father.' That was what Heather said when I got back to Cambridge and unveiled the plan. One friend said our new-born boy had 'wise eyes', while another, a firm believer in reincarnation who reckoned she had been a priest in a previous life, declared he was 'an old soul'. And it was true that he seemed immediately grown-up, mature and sensible, with a balanced, easy-going approach to life. I was the one with irrational demands and urges, clamouring for instant gratification. There wasn't room for both of us at his mother's breast.

One day I confided my deepest, darkest thoughts to Cosimo. He had a one-word solution to my problems. 'Masturbate,' he said.

He told me the story of Inuits (whose name meant 'the People') living in the far north of Canada. During the long, cold, dark winter, if supplies ran out the men would all leave town. Not, as I fondly imagined, to find food for starving mouths, but to avoid *becoming* food. 'They knew that their wives would feed them to the kids. In winter, husbands are just meat on the hoof.'

Cosimo said it was the fear of cannibalism that drove men out of the igloo.

He kept up with the World Cup in the pages of *La Repubblica* and was a fervent admirer of Alberto Tomba. Tomba was a phenomenon, a celebrity in Italy, an egocentric rich kid from Bologna with a house in Cortina who stood apart from the diffident country boys in the team and was known as 'the white fly'. He was built like a weightlifter and went around with a chinful of stubble and a personal entourage of coach, physio, masseur, doctor, serviceman, psychologist, and manager. It was after winning a couple of Olympic slalom titles at Calgary that he acquired the nickname of 'Tomba la bomba'. His explicit credo was 'I want – I do'. But what he didn't do was the *discesa libera* – the 'free fall'. You had to *want* the downhill and he didn't want it. Once you had to do well in the downhill just to qualify for the slalom; now it was a game for specialists.

Cosimo was scathing about downhill. 'It's all over too fast.' He spoke as if every downhill skier was suffering from premature ejaculation. 'Slalom is art, it's creative; all you need for downhill is strong knees and a dispossessed brain.'

I thought slalom was boring, a mere refinement of technique like playing musical scales. Tomba was just a pop-star, a teenage idol, a spoiled overweight brat who went round thumping plastic poles. He should try hitting a tree with his shoulder and see who bounced then.

'It's easy to see you are a total amateur,' said Cosimo.

Downhill had drama, courage, beauty, simplicity. You drop off the side of the mountain and it's the first man to the bottom. It was like Galileo tipping solid bodies off the leaning tower of Pisa. It was the quintessence of skiing, of freedom, of life; it was pure linearity; everything else, turns and traverses, was a digression. The Norwegian word for the high-speed descent was *villom*, or 'wild journey'. It was the most complete and natural of the disciplines, it was the most dangerous and mysterious. The downhill men were like powerboats to the pedalos of the slalomists.

'They're madmen,' Cosimo said. 'They're willing to die for money, to entertain the crowd. Why do you think anyone is watching? They want to see blood, that's why.'

Cosimo condemned Val d'Isère as a soulless exercise in manipulation. I told him I was going to Italy next, to Val Gardena in the Dolomites. 'That's not Italy,' he said, but didn't explain. He didn't think Sicily was Italy either, or Naples, or even Rome, so I didn't take his view too seriously on this point and put it down to regional prejudice.

It was the end of the evening and Cosimo was already cycling away into the rain when I realized I still hadn't asked him the key question.

'How do I ski?' I yelled out after him.

'Downhill,' he called back over his shoulder.

10

WORLD *Cup, 2nd downhill race.* I wrote it down in my notebook over a cappuccino in a roadside café on the long drive up to the Dolomites out of Milan.

That was my first mistake. There were two downhills in Val Gardena and I had already missed the first of them. Before I got to Val Gardena I didn't even know there were two. The first race was due to be held in Argentina and was switched at the last minute. Just as well I didn't fly to Buenos Aires.

Still I ended up in another country. Driving up into the far north-east of Italy I was crossing an invisible frontier. After the autostrada, beyond Bolzano, where the snow lay thick on the trees that flanked the edge of the road, I stopped to pick up a girl hitchhiking. Anna had finished school for the day and was going home to Santa Cristina.

'Italy pleases me,' I said in Italian.

'This is not Italy,' she said in English. 'We do not speak Italian. We speak *Ladin*.'

Val Gardenans, or Gardenesi, had never taken kindly to the Treaty of Versailles after the First World War that sliced off South Tyrol like a sausage and put it on Italy's plate. In the thirties, Italy's crown prince, Umberto di Savoia, had tried to win over the region by going skiing in Val Gardena. Mussolini dispensed with sporting diplomacy and brought in the muscle of an 'Italianization' programme. Still the Tyroleans stuck defiantly to a variety of German, like the Austrians and the Swiss and even some of the French, and wore feathers in their hats and leather shorts in summer.

'We say "Gröden", not Val Gardena.' By the time I dropped Anna off I felt I had just come out of school too. The next town up the winding road, Selva on the map, was referred to locally as Wolkenstein. It was as if the Alpine regions were more closely linked to one another than they were to the countries whose borders they happened, according to the atlas, to occupy. There was a phantasmal Alpine Republic that stood proudly separate from the rest of Europe, unacknowledged politically and geographically.

While Val d'Isère was mapped out along a straight valley and looked as if it had been slotted into place with a spirit level and compasses, Val Gardena (I couldn't shake off the Italian name) had a shaggier, more organic look, like ivy clinging to a wall, spreading out in all directions. I tracked down the press centre, which had been installed in the municipal sports hall.

'Where's your press card?' said the woman behind the registration desk. 'No identification, no pass.'

I needed the pass: it was the open sesame to all doors and guaranteed free access to the mountain. But I didn't have a press card. I wasn't even sure I qualified. Still, I dug out my wallet and riffled through the contents as if to say *I'm sure I put it in here somewhere.*

I had once conned my way through a security police cordon around El Salvador airport and into a press conference marking the return of El Presidente on the strength of flashing my university library card. The man with the moustache and the bristling machine gun snapped it with his finger, handed it back to me, and waved me forward with the muzzle of his Uzzi. I didn't think I'd get away with it twice.

Was it pure chance that my finger came to rest on Callahan's card? It had a picture of a giant wave on it, swallowing up some minuscule human, but it had the look of authenticity and the word 'photographer' printed in bold characters. I fished it out and handed it over.

'OK, Mr Callahan, go over there, please.'

I had my photograph taken then I went back to the woman and she stuck it on a card with Callahan's name and stamped 'photographer'. Then she looped a cord through a hole in the top and held it out to me. 'Wear this around your neck at all times, to avoid complications.'

For once, it was true, Callahan had spared me complications. His card had worked like a charm. And now I had my passport to the slopes. But it was a false passport. The risk was that as soon as Callahan showed up I would be denounced and kicked out of town. On the other hand, it occurred to me as I slithered back to my draughty Fiat Panda across the car park, I had already firmly established my credentials as Mr Callahan, photographer. Maybe Callahan could pass himself off as me. With my new identity dangling from my neck, I was confident I would be able to avoid complications.

By evening the real Callahan still hadn't appeared so I went out to look for someone who could fill me in on the first race. All I knew from a press hand-out was that Franz Heinzer, who had come second in Val d'Isère, had won, and the Norwegian Atle Skaardal was second.

I passed a hotel with music and light and noise coming

out so I went in. A large man in lederhosen stopped me at the door and pointed to a sign which read 'CHIUSO'. It was a big room, the size of a football pitch, and it was full to bursting with rosy-cheeked fair-haired people stuffing themselves and waiters swarming about with hogs heads on platters and foaming quart mugs of beer, while at one end a brass band was playing and someone was yodelling. It was the Austrian team having dinner.

I wandered into a restaurant a few doors away and was flagged down by Jules Lapin and his secretary. Jules wrote for a French daily and had followed the circuit for nigh on twenty years. He was a short man with a square beard and a rounded air of contentment. Jules was famous for his ingenious expenses claims. He put me in mind of the legendary journalist who had once gone out to the Middle East to cover a football match and on his return put in a mighty claim for a camel 'for the purpose of transport in the desert'. When the editor instructed him to hand the animal over he revised the figure upwards to include the cost of the camel's funeral.

I first met Jules in Val d'Isère, where he was parading a brand new pair of red ski boots which he had chiselled out of one of the sponsors in exchange for a mention in his column.

At the sports hall his secretary had been sitting next to him working on another typewriter. I leaned over to see what she was typing and she flung a protective arm across the sheet of paper as if I'd discovered it in the nude.

'I'm writing up some of Jules's work for him,' she said. He was even using his secretary as a secretary.

When I joined him for dinner I knew Jules knew everyone. What I didn't know was he hoarded his knowledge like a miser.

'I hear Heinzer won,' I said.

'Good race,' Jules said.

'What's he like?'

'How much are you paying to know?'

'Skaardal came close though?'

'Atle?' He pronounced the name with the correct Norwegian inflexion, *Otley*. 'Read my article tomorrow.'

When I had his secretary on my own for a moment I asked her if she knew anything about Heinzer and Skaardal. For some reason she told me all about her previous employer instead, an English banker who had opened an account with an Italian girl and was making regular secret deposits. Not even the waiter could be drawn on the subject of great skiers he had waited on.

It was in a café half an hour later that I struck gold at last, in the shape of Patrick Lang and his Dad. To some, Serge Lang was God. He was the man who created the World Cup. He was born in Albertville (the centre of the 1992 Winter Olympics) and moved to the Vosges, which was the first region in France to learn to ski. In those days it had a lot of snow. He was a friend of Arnold Lunn and was a downhill racer in the thirties. He became a war correspondent then a sports correspondent, covering the St Moritz Olympics in 1948. But the outstanding occasions of the Olympics and the World Championships seemed to him too sporadic for the multitude of skiers, spectators, media and sponsors crying out for ski-racing, so he modelled the World Cup system on the cycling and sailing circuits, unifying and extending a handful of classic events in Europe. Conceived twenty-four years before, during a one-off meet at Portillo in Chile, Lang's brainchild had grown into a global conspiracy that stuck pins into the high-altitude map of the world and set down thirty-odd contests on assorted mountain tops from Japan to Alaska and attracted skiers from Egypt to Brazil. The World Cup Committee was no longer an élite club of *aficionados,* it was a multinational business corporation that had connections and did deals.

Serge was massive, he was lined and tanned and pitted. His face looked like something hanging off the outside of Notre Dame, with several centuries of wear and tear etched into it. He had a reputation for toughness. He went round with a minute Yorkshire terrier on his shoulder, like a pirate with a parrot. When it was too cold he popped the dog inside his jacket and a wet nose poked out like a carnation in his lapel.

I asked Serge about Heinzer and Skaardal. 'Are you writing a book?' he said. 'I am writing a book too. All my memories of great skiers. If I tell you and you publish first, people will say that Serge copies Martin.' He finished his coffee, put his dog on his shoulder, and left.

In the oral culture of Hawaii a man with a pen and notepad was an oddity, a freak; in the mountains of Europe, on the other hand, everyone seemed to be writing a book. Arnold Lunn wrote more than fifty, with such titles as *The Mountains of Youth, The Mountains of Memory, The Englishman on Ski, Whither Europe?, Things that Have Puzzled Me, Is Christianity True?* and *Now I See.* His son Peter wrote a novel, *Evil in High Places.* Hemingway rewrote *The Sun Also Rises* up at Schruns in the winter of 1926. While the ocean consummated all desire and blinded you to everything beyond the next wave, the mountain was a gigantic soapbox and pulpit which tempted every passer-by into gazing down on the world and giving of his superior wisdom.

'Don't worry, Mr Martin, he'll never write it,' said

Patrick, 'he knows too much.' For some strange reason of his own Patrick always called me 'Mr Martin'. He was even taller than his father. He had swept-back brown hair streaked with blond which fell down to his shoulders, a mole on his lip, and a white stetson with ear flaps. He looked like a cross between Gérard Depardieu and a polar bear. His hands were the size of cauliflowers. He wrote for *Biorama*, a Swiss ski journal which he owned, and a dozen other newspapers and magazines. In the press room he was always sandbagged behind a bank of computers and telephones and fax machines. On his card it said *Journaliste*, but he was the electronic nerve centre of the whole operation, the man to whom everyone turned. I had the impression that without him there wouldn't be a World Cup any more.

He was about my age, but he watched out for me like a fond father, fixing me up with hotels, getting me out of scrapes. At Val d'Isère he disapproved of my shoes. 'They will kill you,' he said. It was true the soles of my Doc Martens were worn smooth and I had to skate down the path to my hotel. 'You need these,' he said, tapping the corrugated soles of his beaten-up boots. 'And look at this coat, it is far too heavy, it gets saturated.' He got me kitted out with a pair of Timberlands and a purple Patagonia jacket made out of a hydrophobic membrane with nine billion pores per square inch. He made me wind-proof, snow-proof, and sweat-proof. 'That is a serious coat,' he said. 'Now you look like a real mountain man.'

In Val Gardena it was Patrick who granted my wish for knowledge. This was Heinzer's tenth year on the World Cup circuit. He had won a few downhills but yo-yoed up and down the rankings. 'He is a great skier. He always was. But as long as Zurbriggen was around, the Swiss couldn't see beyond their star. Now Heinzer comes out of the shadows.' In the summer he milked cows on his father's farm in the high Alps of Rickenbach. He was a quiet man, known as 'Sunny Boy' for his perpetual smile. Skaardal was part of the Norwegian 'boom'. They were trying to shake off their old image of Nordic skiers – *laufers*, the label Lunn had hung them with – and prove themselves in the Alpine disciplines. 'They want to be ready for Lillehammer in '94,' Patrick said. Norway was gearing up for the Winter Olympics it was hosting only two years after Val d'Isère.

'This book of yours,' Patrick said. 'It sounds great, but you want to know how to make it really interesting?'

'How?'

'Put in plenty of photographs,' he said.

The next morning I phoned Simon in London to tell him everything I had learned. He cut me short. 'Heinzer and Skaardal are old news,' he said. 'That was yesterday. We got all that on Ceefax last night. What we want to know about is today's race.'

11

THE start was overshadowed by the wrathful, wrinkled, ten-thousand-foot-high brow of Sassolungo (or Sasslonch in Ladin), whose bald pate wore a toupee of wind-blown snow. In the summer, climbers clawed up its vertical corrugations. Now, clinging to the bridge of the nose, like Pompeii nestling beneath Vesuvius, a wind-swept marquee provided a fragile shelter for the competitors who queued up for their turn to take the drop. The narrow slit at the front gave an oblique view down on the course ahead and skiers squinted through it like fortune tellers gazing into the crystal ball, trying to figure out their immediate future, or whether they had one.

Unlike athletics, where everyone starts simultaneously, downhill skiers set off at ninety-second intervals, and, within limits, choose their own moment to jump into space. After a count-down – '1 minute, 30 seconds, 15 seconds' – a series of electronic beeps marks out a window several seconds long. You plant your skis over the abyss, rock to and fro, then take a deep breath, thrust forward and shove back the 'magic wand', the thin, hinged baton wired up to trigger the Longines timer. At Val Gardena, immediately beneath the start was a cruel S-bend which dropped off into nothingness; going over the edge was like being flushed away or sliding down the gullet of a python.

Franz Heinzer was wearing the number 10 vest over his fluorescent orange leotard licked by scarlet flames. Sunny Boy wasn't smiling now, he was serious; he was limbering up, writhing like a Mambo dancer between his poles and bouncing his knee off his nose. Then he turned to spiritual exercises. He fell to his knees, praying with his skis on, hands clasped together, murmuring invocations. He had a mop of unruly brown hair and a fresh-faced complexion and even when he frowned he had dimples. He didn't look as if he had anything on his conscience.

Heinzer had skied almost as soon as he could walk. The infant Franz went to school on skis with his older brother and sister. At the age of eleven he was already the star of his local ski club; at fifteen he joined the Swiss national team. He pledged himself to the snow: skiing was a kind of renunciation, a commitment to higher things. He spent two and a half years, from sixteen through to eighteen, just recovering from an injury. Heinzer was the closest thing in downhill to a saint. Now, a decade on from his comeback, with youngsters like Skaardal snapping at his heels, this season was perhaps his last chance of World Cup canonization.

'Don't talk to them at the start,' Patrick had warned me. 'They're liable to snap your head off.'

'Last year, you were second here to Zurbriggen,' I said to Heinzer, deciding to risk it anyway. 'What is the difference this year?'

He gave me one of his disarming grins. 'Zurbriggen retires.'

'Do you have more of an incentive to win?'

'Yes. I open a sports shop. I need to win to sell more ski suits.'

Heinzer crossed himself and vanished into the marquee. A minute or two later he shoved out of the gate, dug in his poles – shaped to hug the curve of his body – then relaxed into a gliding crouch, leaned into the sharp left a couple of hundred yards away at around eighty miles an hour, and dipped out of sight down the hill. He was effortless and light on his skis, passing over the snow like the wind. It was three years since he had fallen in a race in Japan and he seemed to have forgotten that mistakes were possible. He had that quality that Hemingway, writing about matadors, called 'grace under pressure'. Heinzer was the kind of man who wouldn't understand pressure if you drove over him with a tank.

I made my way down gingerly, searching for the ideal spot to view the action from. But you couldn't always get close to the course, and where you could it was often obscured by the edge of the forest and twists in the terrain. All I caught was a split-second technicolour flash of high-velocity Gore-Tex, a Doppler-effect of skis skittering over snow. Only Boris stopped to speak to me. He wasn't planning to, but when a binding gave way and he was skiing on just one ski and a boot, it slowed him down a lot.

Lower down I found a drop where the racers were getting fifty feet of air under their skis. Overlooking the course was a castle that might have been the model for Schloss Adler, the mountain-top fortress in *Where Eagles Dare* where the devious Richard Burton and his ruthless sidekick Clint Eastwood hoodwink the entire SS and get away with the names of all the spies in England.

'Hey, pedestrian, shift your butt out of my frame.' Callahan had a habit of sneaking up on you like the abominable snowman. He hated *pedestrians* – they were the enemy of the sports photographer. His tripod was wedged between a couple of rocks up above the course and he was shooting aerials against the brooding backdrop of the castle. He had parachuted in that morning and stopped off at the press centre.

'They said there was some other photographer called Callahan around. Can you believe that? Couldn't get a pass. I had to hoof it up here like some kind of yak.'

I told him there wasn't that much to see at the top anyhow. He plugged his head back into the lens. A UFO whizzed by and Callahan's camera whirred.

'Did you see that?' I said.

'No. If you see something sharp in the camera, you've missed it.'

'So you're shooting blind?'

'You always are. When you trip the shutter, a mirror pops up inside and blocks your view. You're *creating* a moment, not capturing it. I don't record, I make it happen. You've got to see it in your mind.'

'Didn't you cut it a little fine getting here?' I said.

'I meant to ski the place first. But you can spend days getting to know the mountain and then the world champ flashes by and your camera jams because you've got snow in your motor.'

The mountain could be a vale of tears to photographers. Nature was always jiggling the settings. Even when the snow was good and the weather calm nothing stayed the same for long. You could stake out the perfect location at ten o'clock and an hour later a jutting crag would spill shadow all over it like ink.

Sports photographers tend to specialize: they make a whole career out of snapping surfers or Formula 1 drivers or golfers. Tommy was a tennis photographer who was trying to break the mould. He'd won the title of Sports Photographer of the Year and it had gone to his head. He'd never shot skiers before, but he didn't see why Heinzer should be a tougher proposition than Ivan Lendl. He couldn't ski but then he couldn't play tennis either. When he turned up at Val d'Isère to take pictures for Jules Lapin he was wearing a mackintosh and green wellington boots. He lugged his gear up the hill to the last tight bend on the course, set up his 400 mm F2 lens with the gaping front element and hood, and dug himself in. He hadn't counted on the 'cavalcade', the army of servicemen and course officials who stampede down at the end of the race. As they charged round the last bend their skis gouged up a jet of snow that caked Tommy's camera and added a filter tip to the F2 lens. It took him two days to melt it all out.

For the slalom, Tommy was smart and took the cable-car to the top and edged his way down to the start. Then he lost his footing and tobogganed half-way down the course on his backside, ricocheting off the gates and jeered on by his fellow photographers. That finished him and he never came back.

It was a lucky break for Callahan: Jules took some of his pictures instead. The only trouble was he never paid for them. 'The best shots are taken by the guys who ski best,' Callahan said. 'You've got to be able to move around the mountain.'

It often happened that we would be driving along and Callahan would suddenly slam on the brakes and gesture at some distant pink peak, floating above a doughnut of clouds. 'Check that light!' he would crow. 'When there's cloud in the valley there's still light on the mountain.'

Callahan had once joined an expedition on Acongagua in the Andes – at 24,000 feet the highest summit in all the Americas – and yearned to go back. 'You couldn't breathe, it was almost above the atmosphere, the diamond dust in the air stabbed your face – but you should have seen the light. It was raw sun, clean and pure, bouncing back off the snow, it made everything electric.' He was drawn to high altitudes like a moth to a flame. Because of the fast shutter speeds needed to capture the skier in flight, you had to have more light hitting the lens. But Callahan favoured quality of light over sheer quantity. The highpoint of his day was not noon, but sundown, when the hard lines were softened by shadow and the whiteness was split up and shuffled through the composite shades of the spectrum, producing unexpected combinations and impressionistic tints. His optimal time for shooting was the last moment before it became technically impossible, when the final dregs of daylight were draining from the sky, leaving only a ghostly luminosity peopled by silhouettes.

Callahan was once turned down for a newspaper job. 'You're not a sports photographer,' the editor said after flicking through his portfolio of shots: a grey nothing with a ball passing out of the top right hand corner of the frame; a golfer's eyes, following an invisible drive; the grass of an empty tennis court striated with shadows like a zebra. And it was true, he wasn't: he was a memorialist of the ephemeral and the intangible, more a poet than a photographer. But he eschewed the label of artist. 'Fuck art, let's dance,' he said. It was a kind of manifesto.

Atle Skaardal was first man out of the pen at noon. The number 1 bib is usually seen as a ball and chain round your leg: the true line has not been skied by the forerunners and the piste is still lumpy, not yet racing smooth. None of that seemed to worry him though. It took him exactly two minutes to travel the 3400 yards to the bottom. Then he waited an hour in the finish enclosure, tense and awkward in his heavy boots, closely chaperoned by a man from Blizzard, his ski manufacturers, to see if anyone could go faster.

Skaardal was a slight twenty-four-year old engineering student from Oslo. He thought logically about his skiing, rigorously weighing the nuances of technique, the finer points of the ski – length, edges, wax – and the precise physical conditions of the terrain. He belonged to a highly trained, motivated, amply financed team and a country whose self-esteem hung on reasserting itself over the Alpine nations. At Val d'Isère he was the fastest man through the beam a quarter of the way down before he fell. Determined to leave nothing to chance at Val Gardena, Norwegian technicians had been out on the course the night before the first race, prodding it with stethoscopes and taking the temperature of the snow. Atle and his serviceman calculated the appropriate skis and the wax most exactly suited to a twelve o'clock start, when the sun would still be showing to the east of Sassolungo and warming the snow. But the race was delayed for forty-five minutes after one of the forerunners had fallen, the sun passed behind the rock, and the snow cooled and the Norwegian came in second. When he said afterwards, 'I have a little more to come', it wasn't optimism speaking but only scientific knowledge. He shaved two tenths of a second off his time on the second run.

No one went as fast as the Norwegian Engineer that day. The Swiss Saint was .76 of a second slower and came in fifth. But Val Gardena had settled Heinzer at the top of the World Cup rankings.

12

On the Sunday after the contest, we went round to Steve Lee's hotel. Steve Lee was the lone Australian on the tour. There was a famous photograph of him flying off a jump in Vail, about ten feet in the air, with one of his skis ten inches below his boots on its way down. His binding had given way at the wrong moment. The picture was taken by an obscure photographer from the *Denver Post*. 'It was a fluke shot,' Callahan said bitterly. 'The guy was in the right place at the right time, that's all.'

In 1985 the Australian won a World Cup super-G in Japan. In Val d'Isère he came fifty-second; in Val Gardena he was still several seconds and thirty-odd places adrift of the points earned by the top fifteen. He had a Byronic profile and was twenty-eight years old. At the same age Zurbriggen had already retired.

'If you're Zurbriggen, you can afford to retire,' he said.

Steve Lee had one thing Zurbriggen didn't have – a lip beard. I had never seen anything like it before: a Clark Gable pencil moustache wedged under his lower lip. He thought of it as his good luck charm, the equivalent of the Bell jar. He had been taught to ski by his father in the Australian Alps, sandwiched between Sydney and Melbourne, where skiing began in Australia as far back as the 1850s.

'If he'd been born on the coast he would have been a surfer,' Callahan said. It was his highest compliment.

Steve was watching a video of Tomba in the Giant Slalom at Alta Badia the previous week. Tomba was lying second in the overall World Cup rankings behind Heinzer, but if you didn't ski the downhill you didn't really count. 'His mama won't let him do the downhill,' Lee said. 'Too fast. Too dangerous.' Tomba's parents were in textiles and well connected; they owned a mountain or two and had the money and power to lay down the law, but it wasn't as if Alberto was putting up much of a struggle.

'So what makes the true downhiller?'

'To ski downhill you have to want to let go. The one who wins is the guy who lets go the most. Now look at Tomba.' He was rerunning the tape. 'That's style: he moves so beautifully.' There wasn't a hair out of place in Tomba's entire descent. At the bottom he saluted the cheering crowd and performed a celebratory somersault before being mobbed by photographers, journalists, and fans, all scrambling to touch the hem of his leotard.

Steve gave a grimace of disapproval, almost disgust. 'In downhill, style doesn't matter. You can be stylish and come last, or look terrible and win. You've got to be at the limit of control. Or, better still, completely out of control, but still on your feet. The safest position is the most dangerous. You can't be tentative or cautious – that only gets you into trouble.'

The downhiller just pointed his skis at the bottom and kept going until he ran out of mountain; he only turned where the mountain turned. From his point of view, the slalomist was going in the wrong direction, zigzagging sideways, all but backwards. It was like travelling in reverse gear. The gate system – flexible poles that snapped back when you whacked them with your shoulder – was there to impede the skier's natural movement down the hill, it was a distortion, a disfigurement of the perfect geometry of the straight line.

Whatever slows you down is bad; whatever speeds you up is good. That was why Steve liked Val Gardena. When I came down the day before, I passed through a spray of artificial snow being pumped out of guns stationed along the side of the piste. Given the twenty-odd inches of snow already underfoot, it seemed superfluous. 'Icing on the cake,' said Lee. 'Artificial snow makes for a faster surface. Look at natural snow under a microscope and you'll see air between the crystals; artificial snow has had all the air squeezed out. It's like tarmac instead of cobbles.'

Tomba won the Giant Slalom and earned some ironic cheers from the downhill crowd around the screen. It was the Norwegian, Kjuus, who elicited the loudest gasps of admiration when he managed to stay in the race even after losing his balance a couple of times. 'You can see the difference there all right,' Steve said. 'Tomba is all control. And Kjuus is all abandon: he's surrendered to the force.'

Gravity was like God: invisible, ubiquitous, all-powerful, it was what held the universe together. While climbers made a virtue out of fighting that fatal attraction, skiers yielded body and soul to its embrace. An entire mythology and morality had gathered around the ascent of mountains, but *coming down* had only negative connotations in our archetypes: all variations on the Fall, decline, decadence, the descent of man. Mountaineers tended to sneer at skiers, as Ruskin had once sneered at mountaineers, for treating the mountain as a 'soaped pole in a bear garden'. Climbing was a nineteenth-century substitute for religion, but skiing was a twentieth-century pagan affirmation of earthly existence. It was like falling in love, giving up reason for passion and sacrificing self-control in the name of intensity.

Skiing was about freedom and transgression, pushing back the horizon of the possible. Some skiers had to find places no one had ever skied before to feel free; for Steve Lee it was enough to go completely out of bounds right there on the piste and storm the dark recesses of the mind. What held you back was not so much your equipment or even your physical ability but the boundaries of your thinking.

As Callahan and I were leaving, Steve said to me, 'Don't try and jump the Camels today, whatever you do.'

We tried anyway. Maybe that was what he intended. The 'Camels' were the bumps about two-thirds of the way down the course that were the greatest hazard to the skiers. They consisted of three humps, a bactrian followed by a dromedary. You took off from the first and it depended on your speed and momentum whether or not you made it over the third and were clean away or sliced into the incline and had to stagger up it.

We started together at the top, but I lost Callahan on the way down. I couldn't find the Camels either. They seemed to me like another fictional animal, invented to justify inflated claims. I thought for a while I'd taken the wrong route until I checked the map at the bottom.

'You missed the Camels!' Callahan said. 'That's like walking into MacDonalds and missing the hamburgers.'

The landscape was two landscapes, two quite separate mountains. I had been hiking across a field, through a forest, clambering over a stile and an old wall, and noticing nothing very remarkable about it. He had been overflying the geography in a spotter plane and discovering all the elements that eluded my low-level perception: the hidden contours of prehistoric villages, leylines leading to infinity, alien landing strips, and camels. I had something right in front of my nose, right under my feet, and I couldn't even see it.

'You're looking too hard,' Callahan said. 'This isn't a scientific experiment, it's an *experience*.'

It was the opposite of surfing in Hawaii where I was a kook and couldn't get anything right. In Val Gardena I felt effortlessly in control. And that was just the trouble: I was skiing like Tomba, always within my limits, pansying around with too many turns, wheeling through imaginary gates and keeping the brakes on. I still had to learn how to *surrender to the force*.

The big difference between Steve Lee and me was speed. On some sections of the course he was going over 100 kph. At his velocity the course contracted, formed into recognizable contours and camels; at mine, it stretched out into an interminable roll of Andrex. You could time his descent on a sixty-second stopwatch; for me you needed an alarm clock or a calendar. By the time I got to the bottom I had whiskers and wrinkles.

Of course, we were all living an illusion. I began with a sense of time speeding up and overtaking, leaving me floundering in its wake. His internal chronometer slowed down on his dizzying descent, as if he had been exempted from the passage of time. I remembered something Steve Lee had said: 'I'm doing everything right, only the clock is letting me down.' When the downhillers flashed over the finish line, they pulled up into a tight braking arc, partly to avoid crashing into the barrier dividing the spectators from the course, but partly to be able to crane their necks round and inspect their official time on the electronic scoreboard. After pushing back the magic wand, they had entered a private, secluded time frame, cut off from chronological humanity rooted alongside the piste. So it was that they often shook their heads in disbelief when they returned to the Newtonian universe and found that the second hand had been ticking round all along. As they took off their helmets, they had the otherworldly look of astronauts who had seen things not meant for human eyes and were having difficulty readjusting to terrestrial gravity.

The downhill was like jumping into an empty liftshaft: so long as you were in motion, you had a sensation of weightlessness, as if you were liberated from the force that was sucking you down. It was only when you hit the bottom that the sensation of mass returned with a horrible thud.

I saw Callahan once more in Val Gardena before he headed off for Mundaca in Spain where there was a big swell predicted. We were at the post-race press party in the Palazzo dei Congressi in Santa Cristina. Jules and his secretary were there too. 'I got my money out of Bugs Bunny and my pound of flesh out of his secretary,' Callahan said between mouthfuls of apple strudel. 'You ask her.' Then he was gone.

Callahan had the intensity and transience of a dream. He flickered on and off like a strobe flash, beaming out pulses of energy, fixing the rest of us in rigid poses. He was as unswerving as a dart heading for the fifty. There was no distinction between his thought and his action, his body and his mind. I wore Callahan's name around my neck, but I still wasn't Callahan. He was there to avoid complications, to banish ambiguity and doubt. It wasn't just that he did things I didn't do, it was that he did them unshadowed by anxiety or remorse. He was my anti-conscience, cursing me for inertia, for doors I never opened and roads I never travelled.

13

ELJA Renfree was the official statistician of the World Cup and keeper of the computers; unofficially she was camp confidante. 'I can tell you everything you want to know about everyone,' she said when Patrick Lang introduced me to her at the party. 'Who, when, where, and how long.' It was a tempting offer. We left together and found a café where she ordered two cappuccinos and drank them in tandem.

Elja used to ski for Holland, but had wrecked her right knee years before when she fell in a race in Switzerland. There was a thaw, followed by a freeze, and Elja had been locked into the frozen tramlines of another skier. When she tried to turn left the tracks turned right and her own momentum brought her down. The way she described it was 'getting caught in a rut'.

Now she couldn't turn any more.

'Perfect for downhill,' I said.

'I tried it once. I forgot that you have to turn to brake.'

In a way Elja was the archetypal downhiller: the only way she could brake was to fall. But she had gone beyond skiing: now she explored the mountains of the mind. When she talked a crescent of brown hair swung down over her eyes and curtained her gaze from reality.

She had married when she was twenty-one and divorced a year later. It was then she decided to change her name to Renfree. Her maiden name was Boerman.

The name of her husband was Hedeman. She was fed up with names that had 'man' in them, and wanted something that was simple and meaningful. 'After being married, I wanted to symbolize my freedom. *Rennen* in Dutch means run. So the name really means Runfree. And that was what I was doing – running free.'

I thought that was a genuinely inspirational name and said I wouldn't mind adopting it myself.

'There was a Max Renfree,' Elja said. 'He was my first analyst.'

She laughed. 'Do you think that's crazy?' She could appreciate the irony of wanting a name that signified a glorious independence, and borrowing it from another man. She had run away from him, too, in the end, but clung to his name. Maybe all skiers were this way: staking a claim for freedom while locked into a pattern of dependence and repetition.

I said it was too bad she couldn't ski any more.

'I still ski in my dreams though,' she said.

'You dream about skiing?'

'I dream about everything. You want dreams? I've got a ten-year catalogue of them, all computerized. Tell me what you want and I'll look it up in my index.'

Snow was drifting in soundless slow motion through the night as she led me back to her room in the Hotel Christiania to consult her dream file. She kept a pad by the side of the bed to record her dreams the moment she woke up (or rather, she woke in order to record them). On the cabinet next to it was a book, *A Soul's Journey*, a first-person account of life on the astral plane.

The dreams were stored on her Toshiba T1000 portable computer.

'I have hard copy though,' she said, digging into a

trunk and coming up with a thick folder. 'These are only the ones I've typed up. I've got masses of hand-written ones. Do you want to see them too?'

'Are you sure you don't mind me looking at this?' I felt like I was inspecting someone's underwear.

'No, I *want* you to look at it,' she insisted.

I sat down and started to read.

I discovered that Elja and I had a lot in common: we both robbed banks and had science fiction adventures and flew in strange machines. She died many times: eaten alive by aliens or blown up by her mother or sucked into a whirlpool. She is raped by a snake; volcanoes erupt; earthquakes, tombs, wolves, whales. She goes driving in a caravan with Prince Charles. She is a successful writer who has to escape from her fans in a balloon. She meets God and has a wonderful revelation but can't remember what it is. One of her dreams started: 'I am a mass-murderer.' Another ended on the line, 'I wait for dementia to set in.'

Her skiing dreams were fabulously eventful, with people soaring uphill and falling down ravines. Perhaps in one way or another all her dreams were about skiing. The last in the file, dated within the last week, concerned mountains and gods. The first, dating from her early teens, had snow in it.

This is what I read on the first page:

DREAMS

EARLY TEENS (writing this up from memory. Had used the dream as material for an essay, which the teacher warned me not to do in future, as people can tell all sorts of things about you from your dreams.) Am escaping across the snow with papa. A black cloaked horseman with a black dog catches up with us easily, and starts to rub the passenger window, heating it up so it starts to melt. We get away or he lets us go. We are in a hotel with long corridors and wooden floors. I have locked my bedroom door, but I hear the horse's hooves outside the door. The rider tries the lock, but can't get in. I can hear the dog scratch and sniff at the door. The next day we ski again over the snow. We are tired, and are pleased to find some steps leading down to somewhere to stay the night. We go inside to find the horseman waiting for us behind the counter, checking guests in. I feel a sense of hopelessness or surrender. We can't escape him, and he has won.

I said it reminded me of certain stories by Kafka, where you are pursued by some inexorable force for reasons you don't understand. But Elja understood. She deciphered the dream according to a canonical code: animals stood for instinctive drives; snow for emotional frigidity.

I climb up a mountain and enjoy the speed of coming down. But the snow is melting and I keep hitting rocks.

This was her most frequent type of skiing dream.

'What do you think that means?' I asked.

'Skiing is something to do with mastery, isn't it? When the snow melts it undermines the whole thing. It's to do with being a wonderful being and then not.'

We turned to the last page of the folder.

I go up a mountain in a cable-car. There are two stops on the way, but you can't get out at the first as there is nowhere to stand. When I get out at the second, highest

> stop I look out on to mountains higher still. On the crest, outlined against the sky, is a golden statue of Apollo. Near the lift there is an image – set in the rock – of Dionysus holding a Narcissus flower. A voice tells me he was never intended to rule over anything but animals. I am filled with a sense of dread. I sense he will demand retribution or revenge.

Apollo was her father, a respected biochemist who was very strict at home. Her friends were afraid to come into the house. So were her mother's friends. A flash of inspiration lit up her face. 'Of course,' she said, slapping herself on the forehead, 'Apollo is the sun-god. He is the one who melts the snow and stops you in your tracks. It's the same with Icarus – you want to fly and he burns your wings off.'

'So the downward motion is the Dionysian spirit in action?'

'You want to let go – and go down – but you still need the Apollonian to oversee things and harness the force – to make it into an art. You want to let the Dionysian spirit rip, but you want control too.' She paused. 'Is that a contradiction?'

'Yes and no,' I said.

Elja pulled a book out of her trunk. It was Jung's *Memories, Dreams, Reflections*. She had used a yellow marker pen to highlight significant passages; sometimes there was no white left on the page. She referred me to a chapter in which Jung is staying with Pueblo Indians in America:

> 'Do you not think that all life comes from the mountain?' An elderly Indian had come up to me, and asked me this

heaven knows how far-reaching question. A glance at the river pouring down from the mountain showed me the outward image that had engendered this conclusion. Obviously, all life came from the mountain, for where there is water, there is life. Nothing could be more obvious. In his question I felt a swelling emotion connected with the word 'mountain', and thought of the tale of secret rites celebrated on the mountain. I replied, 'Everyone can see that you speak the truth.'

For Elja the World Cup was the stage for a series of sacred rituals, a fertility dance of some sort, a quest for the source of life. The downhill was a twentieth-century invention, but it harked back to ancient pagan traditions. The mountain was the symbol of the collective unconscious, the origin of the *prima materia*, the alchemical conjunction of opposites.

On another page Elja showed me a diagram of a mountain drawn up by the Cabbalists. Inside the pyramid was a temple, and inside the innermost sanctum, the holy of holies, was the philosopher's stone, the key to all knowledge. In the background was the zodiac, and in the foreground a blindfolded man.

14

COSIMO seemed disappointed to see me. 'You ought to be dead by now. What went wrong?'

On Monday the white circus took down its tents and trooped off for Christmas. There wasn't another World Cup contest until the New Year. Cosimo was in Italy for the vacation, so we agreed to go skiing together in Monte Rosa. From peak to peak it was only a couple of hundred miles away, but I had to drive double that, south to the motorway, west to Turin, then north again.

Like Hans Castorp in Thomas Mann's *Magic Mountain*, Cosimo had once spent an entire season in a Swiss sanatorium high above Davos. He wasn't ill though, he didn't have shadows on his lungs: the sanatorium had been turned into a hostel for skiers and he was giving lessons. In the chapter entitled 'Snow', Mann puts his idealistic, romantic, consumptive, pre-First-World-War hero on a pair of oak skis. The snowfall that winter is 'monstrous and immeasurable' and provides a foretaste of easeful death. On the misty February day that Castorp slides surreptitiously out, flouting sanatorium rules, irresistibly drawn to the snowy desolation, the thermometer shows ten to fifteen degrees of frost.

He takes the funicular up the Schatzalp and loses himself in the loneliest part of the mountain, far from pedagogues and hypochondriacs. Castorp enjoys the cold. He wears only his long-sleeved camelhair waistcoat and breeches. He wants to encounter nothing but the inorganic on his path, nothing but the wintry solitude of the lifeless mountain. He goes up and up, further than he has gone before, until the forest and the town below are lost from sight beneath the clouds. Beyond the whisper of his own skis on the powder, everything is silence. Nothing moves, not a bird sings, not a branch twitches beneath its heavy burden. Castorp rushes down inclines he can barely see, skilled enough to leave parallel tracks behind him, using the Telemark turn – one leg forward, the other bent at the knee.

When he comes upon a deserted wooden hut the light is fading and the snow is falling more heavily. So he turns his skis round and vanishes into the dim vastness where the white earth merges with the white sky. There are no more landmarks, no trees or houses, no path to guide him, but his skis are like homing pigeons, they know the way back. He travels with infinite care, clambering over rocky outcrops browsing like dinosaurs in the gathering gloom, and edging down, always thrusting forwards through the choking blinding snow, chasing shadows that might be clumps of pines.

When he glimpses the silhouette of a building below him, he abandons himself to the slope and twists to a halt by the same lonely hut that he left behind almost an hour before. There can be no mistake. Here are his own tracks, pointing away, almost buried, and now completed by the lines leading back again. The bad light and snow have thrown out his mental compass and he has come full circle. It is geometrically impossible: he is sure he has gone down, but somehow he has got back up again as if he were going round and round an Escher staircase. The wind sweeps cornflakes of snow into his mouth. Castorp unhooks his skis and twiddles the door-latch uselessly and takes a pull from a flask of port while the warmth retreats from the extremities of his body.

A manifesto by Salvador Dali defined the surrealist in terms of for and against. Under the 'for' column he put *magic, soft watches, me*; under 'against', *medicine, history, men*. One of the things he was for was *coastlines*; another he was against was *mountains*. The pattern of waves crashing against the shore was ceaselessly changing; the mountain was invariable. The sea was unfathomable, dark, mysterious, shifty; the mountain was a massive amplification of clarity and solidity. Water meeting earth on the one hand, all fluidity and erosion; unbending stone, rock, sheer hardness on the other. Waves – all transience and illusion – were like an ironic parody of mountains in their power and permanence. In Dali's equation, mountains were on the same side as men; they were a metaphor of masculinity – erect, intransigent, muscular, immovable – while the yielding coastline was feminine in character.

But Thomas Mann saw no necessary antithesis between mountainside up above and seaside down below. Snow, after all, is just a crystalline form of water, precipitated at a certain temperature and in the right conditions of humidity. Its presence transforms the mountain into a frozen cataract. Here there is no thunder of surf, but Castorp feels the same awe and terror that the swollen North Sea once aroused in him.

So it is that when he crams himself up against the wall under the overhanging eaves and falls asleep Hans Castorp dreams of a beautiful bay and islands and a beach shaded by the rustling fronds of palm trees.

Laughing children caper down to the warm southern ocean and plunge into the welcoming waves and are carried away on them like magic carpets. A young mother presses her breast to her baby's mouth. The world is good, it glows with goodness, it perspires goodness. Then Hans is beckoned by a boy into a towering temple and within its cold, shadowy depths witnesses two withered old hags dismembering a child. Hans tries to run away, but there is no way out of the temple and he collides with columns of stone.

Castorp wrestles himself to his feet, pushes his boots into his toe straps, and stamps his feet. It has stopped snowing, the wind has died and moonlight glints on pink ridges. The skier lets the mountain take him where it will and he returns safely to the sanatorium.

Even while he is still lying in the snow, Hans Castorp interprets his dream as a mystic immersion in the universal, as a vision of ultimate truth:

> Now I know that it is not out of our single souls we dream. We dream anonymously and communally, if each after his fashion. The great soul of which we are a part may dream through us, in our manner of dreaming, its own secret dreams, of its youth, its hope, its joy and peace – and its blood sacrifice.

15

COSIMO thought that all downhillers deserved to die: it was part of the logic of what they were doing and their descent was incomplete without it. You couldn't expect to escape if you repeatedly flung yourself into the jaws. He drew my attention to a headline in *La Repubblica,* TUTTI MORTI SOTTO LA NEVE and nodded with grim satisfaction.

'Viva Tomba!' he added. He predicted that Tomba would win the overall World Cup, since Heinzer clearly would not survive the season.

On that Tuesday in December Cosimo's idea was to get right away from the trail and the resort, from ski-lifts and the madding crowd. He didn't want recreation, he didn't want sport on well-tracked terrain, he wanted to wrestle with the untamed mountain like one of those nineteenth-century muscular clergymen who marched about the Alps before the days of tunnels and planes and escalators to heaven. Perhaps it was the fault of studying criminology, but Cosimo thought of the plain as a place of sin and pollution. For years he had complained of being slowly poisoned in Cambridge; when his rooms on the site of Cavendish's atom-splitting experiments were diagnosed as radioactive his fears were triumphantly vindicated. Only in the hills, far above the sea-level atmosphere of society, could he open up his lungs, expel the sickness, and give rapturous utterance: '*Che bello!*'. Monte Rosa was Cosimo's Alpine Shangri-La, a serene upland paradise quarantined half-way between earth and sky, where time stretched out into eternity. Monte Rosa was his snowdome. It was Cuvier, Cosimo said, who first demonstrated that there are fewer microbes at higher latitudes by suspending buckets of decomposing hay and urine from a balloon.

We took the funicular then cut off east across the mountain, leaving behind us the familiar cluttered pistes, and traversed up to a ridge. We flung ourselves across a deserted bowl, under a flying buttress of ice, and out on to a brittle parapet. Cosimo pointed out a pair of parallel lines scarring an otherwise unblemished face high above us which was taking the full force of the sun.

Callahan liked to take pictures of tracks in the snow. Cosimo would examine them closely like a hunter scrutinizing hoofprints. Ski tracks were the traces of your personal fall line, but they were more than a signature. Properly construed, these patterns – clean tramlines, sinuous figures-of-eight, dotted rhythms – were a syntax, an entire narrative, the outward manifestation of a psychology, as redolent of history as a battlefield after the clamour of war has ceased. They were the tranquil imprint of intense emotion, the archives of legend.

'You see there,' Cosimo said, 'that was a failed suicide attempt. The mountain must have been asleep. Now it is awake. We must tread lightly.'

To most people, a mountain is as rough and tough as a well-built Hercules; to Cosimo it was as sensitive as a baby. Sometimes a whisper sufficed to set it off. It was a pack of cards you had only to blow on to bring tumbling down. Cosimo didn't so much ski as tiptoe, as if he were treading on a minefield. He hated taking unnecessary risks. 'You have to have the guts to go back,' he said.

As an Alpine guide, Cosimo had seen many deaths on the mountain, but he had never lost one of his own flock. The training film he had watched during his apprenticeship was shot by a Walt Disney cameraman and contained unique footage of an avalanche actually hitting the camera; only the camera itself was found. 'People get mesmerized, paralyzed,' he said, 'like rabbits in the glare of headlights.'

There were different kinds of avalanche to worry about. There was the wet kind, in warm weather, that starts like a snowball and indiscriminately rolls up rocks and trees in its path until it is the size of the Albert Hall, the consistency of cement, and weighs a trillion tons. There was the dry kind, that sends down an explosive shock wave in front and travels faster than a skier, clocking up as much as 190 mph. And there was the slab kind, that snaps off with a loud retort in a single chunk and splinters as it accelerates and could be as wide as the mountain. There were new snow and old snow avalanches, powder, ice and mixed avalanches. I could try to ski round them, or I could try to outrace them, but the chances were I wouldn't make it. Cosimo gave me tips on what to do when it hit: throw away my poles, release my skis, swim towards the light, dig out a breathing space, then keep still – I would use less oxygen that way – and pray for a St Bernard. 'There is nothing random about nature,' he said. 'It is pure cause and effect.'

The greatest recorded avalanche in history occurred in the Andes of northern Peru, on an extinct volcano, the 22,205 foot Huascarán. On 10 January 1962 a chunk of the summit ice-cap measuring 2,800,000 cubic yards broke away. The resulting *huayco* travelled a distance of nine miles, obliterated six villages, partly destroyed another three, and killed more than 6,000 people. The river Santa in the valley below rose by twenty-six feet.

One of the smallest of all avalanches had once embarrassed Cosimo himself. 'It was a miserable thing,' he said, 'barely a few metres wide.' It happened in late spring, almost summer, while he was climbing down an easy slope. The snow had a chequered past, melted and re-frozen a hundred times since it fell months before in weightless flakes, now grey with dust and pebbles. Unheralded by any dramatic clap of thunder, it began to slide, no foaming cataract this but a quiet stream of wet, heavy snow, trickling down the mountainside at no more than ten miles an hour. It was a pleasant sensation to be borne along, without skis, as if on an escalator. But there was no getting off. When he tried to use his axe as a brake the snow walled up behind him and propelled him downward again, pramming him dreamily towards the edge of the ice-cliff and the crevasse below. Gradually Cosimo punted his way to one side of the flow, like a boat scrambling for the bank before it can be dragged over a weir. A hundred metres from the brink, he thrust his blade into a firm drift of snow and held on with both hands. The advancing avalanche nearly yanked his arms from their sockets before it proceeded, serene and unhurried, over the precipice and fanned out into the void beyond. 'Never underestimate the power of snow,' he said.

Cosimo thought of avalanches as a nemesis that wrongdoers bring upon themselves, a form of divine retribution. In the last chapter of *A Moveable Feast*, recalling the winter of 1925–6, Hemingway too suggests that this way of dying is our personal responsibility:

> The first big loss was over the mountains from our valley, in Lech in the Arlberg. A party of Germans wanted to come and ski with Herr Lent on their Christmas vacations. Snow was late that year and the hills and mountain slopes were still warm from the sun when a great snowfall came. The snow was deep and powdery and not bound to the earth at all. Conditions for skiing could not be more dangerous and Herr Lent had wired the Berliners not to come. But it was their vacation time and they were ignorant and had no fear of avalanches. They arrived at Lech and Herr Lent refused to take them out. One man called him a coward and they said they would ski by themselves. Finally he took them to the safest slope he could find. He crossed it himself and then they followed and the whole hillside came down in a rush, rising over them as a tidal wave rises. Thirteen were dug out and nine of them were dead. The Alpine ski school had not prospered before this, and afterwards we were almost the only members.

Cosimo and I took a bus together from one end of the Val d'Aosta to the other, along roads that had become tunnels through the snow. It was a ride that should have taken an hour, but the driver made it in half the time. 'This man is a maniac,' Cosimo said as we hurtled around hairpin bends and skirted the edge of infinite drops. Several times he got up to speak to the driver, but the driver was deaf to Cosimo's entreaties and kept his gaze fixed intently on the road ahead and his foot pressed down on the pedal. Cosimo didn't believe in God, but he crossed himself anyway.

'What is wrong with you?' Cosimo asked the driver as he got down from his cab. 'Why were you driving as if the devil were after you? You could have killed us all.'

'It is the mountain,' said the driver, looking over his shoulder. 'I know it is going to get me. So I drive as fast as I can to give it as little opportunity as possible.'

We had coffee to warm us and steady our nerves. The driver's name was Salvatore. He was a giant of a man and about our age, but when he took off his hat he had no hair beneath it, and his baldness added to his hunted air. As we drank we talked and he seemed to feel he owed us an explanation.

'When I was a boy my father was lost on the mountain in an avalanche. His body was never recovered.'

'Ah,' I nodded, 'the death of a father in childhood is very traumatic.'

'No,' he said. 'I was too young to care. I hardly noticed that he died. People always said I looked like my father but I could barely remember him. My mother brought me up and my older brothers taught me to ski. I loved the mountain and felt at home there. I never had an accident. So long as I stayed on the mountain, I was invulnerable.'

'But . . .'. Cosimo slapped a hand across my mouth.

'Then one day I was out skiing on my own. I had skied the mountain a thousand times, ten thousand, but always there is more to discover and it is ever changing. It was snowing and the wind was blowing hard and I lost my way. I came down a track that was unfamiliar to me and seemed to go on and on. It led me into a kind of tunnel. It was sheltered from the snow so I stopped to get my breath. There was a strange blue light which seemed to come out of the walls. The walls were mainly ice and you could see through them like thick glass. On one side, there was a shadow deep within. I couldn't make out what it was, but I thought it must be an animal of some sort, trapped in the snow, a sheep perhaps. I hacked away at the ice with my pole. It took me a long time. When I was nearly through, I knelt down and stuck my head through the hole I had made. Do you know what I saw?'

He shivered at the memory. Neither of us said anything.

'I saw my own face.' It was the face of his father, perfectly preserved in the ice, like a prehistoric mammoth. After twenty-five years had passed, and he had attained the age at which his father had died, the son had found the missing body. The gaping face that was Salvatore's face but also his father's seemed to reflect his own emotions and its glazed, ageless eyes were wide open with terror. Salvatore recoiled and fled from the tunnel, skiing madly as if there was an avalanche behind him.

'I could never bring myself to go back and no one else could find the tunnel. Perhaps it vanished again in the storm. They said I must have imagined it, but I know what I know.'

As if in a crystal ball, he had seen his own death foretold. 'Now you know why I drive so fast.'

'He is not running away from his destiny,' Cosimo said when we were on our own, 'he is running towards it.' Salvatore was like Oedipus who was put out on the bare hill to die, but lived and flew screaming into the arms of the fate the oracle had predicted. 'One day Salvatore will run into trouble at the crossroads,' Cosimo declared solemnly.

16

It was the second week in January and someone had built a snow dragon on Lammas Land. It was strange enough for a picture of it to appear in *The Times*. For once, the snow had followed me back to Cambridge. You ran into people wearing skis to get around. 'You know what they say in Italy when it's like this?' said Raffaele, the owner of my local café, over the hissing of the Gaggia. *'It's snowing money.'* The New Year was heralded by such miracles.

The 'Kandahar', the fourth downhill of the World Cup season, was in Germany. At least, that's where it was scheduled to take place. In Garmisch-Partenkirchen, an hour's drive out of Munich in the Bavarian Alps, FIS and the local director of tourism were wavering between bouts of positive thinking and despair. The race had been cancelled the last three years in a row for lack of snow and now the big December fall was wearing thin in the warm weather beneath bursts of sleet and drizzle and course officials were dusting down the new snow cannon, installed at a cost of £1.9 million, at the lower end of the slope. If it didn't melt there was the alternative danger that the top crust would freeze and then slide off and leave the hill bare. The German course was like an ancient canvas that cracked and faded in ordinary light and had to be patiently, painstakingly restored.

When the rain came down, Patrick Lang put a brave face on it. 'This is falling as snow above 1300 metres,' he said. The trouble was the race finished at 740 metres: that still left a long way to walk.

In the hotel Leiner the Callahan-Martin team was wedged between the Japanese and the Canadians. I wanted to have a word with Tsuyoshi Tomii and find out how he was getting on, but the entire Japanese squad appeared at breakfast in a phalanx, bowed courteously, and retreated *en masse*. Tsuyoshi was as elusive as gas and wafted silently about the corridors. I didn't need to have a conversation with the Canadians, they communicated, very loudly, through the walls, at all hours of the night.

'What do you fucking want, sucker?'

'Haven't you ever heard of flushing the fucking toilet?'

'Hey, fatso, where's my sock?'

For a while they had tried to shake off their reputation as 'Crazy Canucks', but the name stuck and now they said you needed to be crazy anyway. They still had a pioneering, frontier spirit. One of the Canadians had bought a camera and he was testing it out taking pictures from odd angles of the toilet bowl in his bathroom. I could hear him clambering up the wall.

Brian Stemmle had done as much as anyone to keep up the image. He was known as a 'loose' skier, fearless and capable of anything, with a natural feel for the snow, knowing by instinct where to lay on his edge and where to lay off and glide. He was a party animal who regularly evaded curfew and a practical joker who tipped buckets of water over people while they were in bed. He was the chief lunatic on a team of madmen. He was cocky, he didn't train hard enough, he was laid back.

But he was accorded as much respect as a holy relic or someone who has come back from the dead. He had come back from Kitzbühel. What happened to him there had earned him the title of 'the wishbone man'. People still pulled out the video from time to time and watched it with the same horror and fascination as *Jaws* or *Nightmare on Elm Street*.

In January 1989, Kitzbühel hosted two back-to-back downhills on the Hahnenkamm. In the first, on the Friday, Stemmle finished twenty-first. He decided he had been too tight, too conservative, too cautious. He would let loose in the second. After recovering from knee surgery the summer before, he was feeling as good as he'd ever felt. He made it through the Steilhang traverse, but he was barely in control and carrying too much speed. He slid wide, too wide, on the tight right-hand exit turn. For fifty yards, he was bumping along the left-hand gutter between the piste and the perimeter fence. Then his hand caught in the netting, slewing him round sideways, then his left ski caught, trapping his leg and chopping his speed from 100 km per hour to zero. Equal and opposite forces strove to tear him apart, as if he had been bound to the bowed trunks of a pair of trees and someone had put a knife to the ropes. He was airlifted to Innsbruck, where they pumped gallons of blood into him and kept him on life-support for a week. 'Take heed to yourselves that ye go not up into the mount, or touch the border of it: whosoever toucheth the mount shall be surely put to death,' Jehovah warned the Israelites. That was the Hahnenkamm. It was the abode of the gods and out of bounds to mortals. Breaking the taboo entailed some sacrifices.

Now Stemmle was back again and looking to get even,

talking of the downhill as 'a battle between Man and Nature' and conscious that 'if you sit back or tense up then the hill takes advantage.'

'Some people in your shoes would be looking for a safer job,' I said. 'Shark-wrestling for instance.'

'I guess I'm not "some people",' Stemmle said. He was stocky and fair-haired. Only eighteen months after crashing out, he won the downhill of the inaugural Pan-American Winter Games. At Val d'Isère he was placed tenth. He played down the accident and rejected the 'wishbone' label. 'Some people see my comeback as a kind of miracle. But racing is what I was brought up to do. A downhill course is where I feel most at home.'

We were sitting in the lounge of the Leiner on Saturday night after the race, drinking coffee by the fire, competing for the attention of Suzanne and Sonia, students from Kitzbühel who followed the World Cup around two or three countries for the month of January. They had seen Stemmle take the fall on the Hahnenkamm and stared at him as if hypnotized. 'He is our hero,' they chorused. Suzanne was supposed to be studying journalism, but she rejected my offer of a first-hand account of great moments in sports reporting and private lessons.

'We had our own doc – if not for that he wouldn't have made it,' Glenn, the Canadian manager, confided. 'He had only a forty per cent chance of pulling through.' Glenn wore metal-toed cowboy boots. He had streaks of grey in the curls that sprouted from the open collar of his shirt.

The Canadian team always had a doctor along, or rather a string of doctors working month-long shifts. Nick, the current medic, was a new boy. 'The only time

I've had to do anything I inflicted the injury myself. I tackled a guy in a football game and had to send him off for treatment.'

The Canadians were their own worst enemies. In a sense all their wounds were self-inflicted, they all volunteered for the front line, no one forced them to do what they were doing. They tied a blindfold over their own eyes and walked the plank of their own initiative. But that didn't stop them complaining about being out on a limb. Skiing was still a minority sport in Canada. Most of the top athletes were siphoned off by ice hockey and the sport was starved of funds. 'Unless you're winning medals, people aren't interested.' But unless people got interested, they never would win any medals. They were in a jam. 'We've got the snow, but no facilities,' Glenn said. 'Miles and miles of glaciers and no way of getting to them. We have to be helicoptered into camps.' The Rockies had good skiing, but a small population; the East had a big population but small mountains. Stemmle was the only man on the team from the East.

Even curling was bigger in Canada than Alpine skiing. 'That's not a sport,' Glenn objected, 'it's just an excuse for drinking.'

'Yeah, but at least you can make a living out of it,' said the doc, who claimed that Canada had won more world championships in curling than anything else.

All the Canadians were self-conscious about being Canadian. They were always being compared to the States, especially by themselves. 'Take Kuwait,' Glenn said, 'we've got a lot of armaments over there. Couple of speedboats and a Cessna. The ferry service back home is the shits since they sent that boat out. We're not a great war nation.'

'Let's face it,' said the doc, 'we're not a great *anything* nation. The thing about Canadians is they don't win things. They're destined for mediocrity. Canada just doesn't work as a nation.'

'You want to know the real trouble with Canada?' One of the coaches, Germain, a tall, thin man with a thin black moustache, was waxing philosophical. 'The Chinks. I looked up Wong in the phone directory once. There are pages of 'em. That's what's *wong* with the country. They're taking over. They were OK when they were digging railways and pressing clothes and cooking chop suey; now they're our fucking landlords. We ought to ship 'em back again – in junks. You want to know the only good thing to come from the East? The *sun*.' It was a classic reflex gesture. You were having a hard time; someone must be to blame. You were marginal with respect to mainstream culture; you looked for someone else to marginalize. If you didn't want to be a scapegoat, you found one to take your place.

The Canadian team had spent October in Chile. Germain reckoned it was the best country in South America. They paid their debts and the army was friendly. 'Pinochet was ruthless, but he brought control. I feel kind of an asshole for saying this, but – a little cruelty is no bad thing.' I began to understand why a lot of people went through life without a coach.

'Brian didn't make any mistakes,' Glenn said, 'he just pushed the limits too hard and got caught in the net.' Stemmle was the virgin chosen to be fed to the dragon. And now he was going back again. But there was talk of a 'conversion' and 'rebirth': no more buckets of water and skiving off.

'Now don't get the idea I've gone out and found the

Lord or anything,' Stemmle said, laughing. 'But I did have a bit of a conversation with Him after my crash. I realized then that I was given this very special gift. And when I fell, He said: "I gave this to you, and now I'm going to teach you a lesson. If you don't smarten up, you can forget about it".'

The Hahnenkamm was his penance; he prostrated himself to atone for his sins.

'I've thought a lot about the accident and I've come to realize that everything happens for a reason. I have a much better appreciation of life now.' Stemmle wasn't content with just living and dying any more, he wanted to know why. His game had become more mental than physical, it was metaphysical, and he was worrying over keeping his positive images dominant.

But as soon as he elbowed aside the magic wand, he went into regression: 'When I push out of the start gate, all those thoughts are behind me and I concentrate totally on just one thing: going fast. If you think too much on race day, you're not going fast. If you're thinking about turning in the spot where you're supposed to, by the time you think about it, it's gone by and you're in the net. You don't have time to think – your body has to do the thinking for you.'

When Stemmle was hurtling down the slope, he was conscious of his unconscious and his body took over from his brain. Perhaps that was the sin he was being punished for: rehabilitating the repressed. He left with Suzanne and Sonia to go to a disco.

It didn't do him any good. On Saturday God taught him another lesson. Garmisch was a technical course, very tight, very icy, and he took the wrong line, missed a gate, and was disqualified along with two more crazy

Canucks. It was a gesture of resignation when he pulled off a perfectly executed helicopter spin going over the last jump a hundred metres from the finish. That won a roar of approval from the thousands of spectators, starved of World Cup action for three whole years.

The race was exceptionally tight too, with the first twelve finishers all within three-quarters of a second of one another, and three ties for second, fourth and sixth places. Franz Heinzer stayed on top of the downhill with an eighth, but Skaardal, in joint second, was closing the gap and was just four points behind. I sent off my report to London about another Swiss, Daniel Mahrer, winning the Kandahar, describing him as 'the world's fastest plumber'. As it turned out I had been misinformed: he was a bricklayer before he went into downhill, but he had the battered look of an all-in wrestler. His bruising no-holds-barred run wasn't beautiful to watch, but it worked. Mahrer threw a post-race press party at his hotel. 'Before the Swiss speak only of Zurbriggen,' he said. 'Now maybe they have other names.'

Patrick said it was a throwback to the days when the 'old heroes' were intent on having a good time and the races were just a pretext. 'Now they go to bed at nine – it was not always like this. Women used to queue up. Mahrer, he does not go to bed at nine o'clock.' The consensus view was that you had to be immaculate to win a downhill, and infallible to take the World Cup title: one minuscule miscalculation, a fractional error in line, a wobble of the skis, and suddenly you drop twenty places or you're out of the race. Fool around the night before and you've had it. Patrick had an alternative theory: 'If you are perfect you lose. To win you cannot be an angel – you must be the devil.'

But Mahrer was already looking forward to the next race a week later, with respect to which everything that went before was simply a prelude and a preparation. 'That sets me up for the Hahnenkamm,' he said. 'Kitzbühel is the one. Here you're just the best downhiller this day. Win the Hahnenkamm and you're the best in the world.'

17

HANGING on the wall in the lobby of the Leiner was a photograph of four young women. It wasn't a Callahan shot: there was no action, no blurred limbs and spumes of foam or snow. The four women, all on skis, had their arms around each other's shoulders and they were grinning and laughing at the camera. In the background was a mountain and a flagpole. The flag, frozen in time, was a swastika.

The caption identified the four as Christl Cranz, Heidi Pfeffer-Lanschner, Lisa Resch, and Kathe Grasegger. They were Germany's women's team at the 1936 Winter Olympics, which were held in Garmisch-Partenkirchen. In fact, Garmisch-Partenkirchen didn't exist before those Olympics. Before there was only Garmisch and Partenkirchen. Hitler ordered the two towns to unite as a symbol of the joining together of nations. It was the first time the Alpine disciplines of downhill and slalom had been included in the Olympics.

The women's team had stayed at the Leiner; the men were at the other end of town. Every year there was a reunion at the hotel. It took place in October, so I had missed it for this year, but the man at the front desk told me that Kathe Grasegger still lived in Partenkirchen.

The broad white house in Wildenauer Strasse was hidden away behind a tall hedge and a green gate. In 1936 Kathe Grasegger was eighteen years old, the youngest member of the team, and worked on her parents' farm. Now she was in her seventies, but there was still something of the pig-tailed milkmaid about her. She had white hair and huge blue eyes shadowed by heavy eyebrows, and strong, expressive hands. She had learned to ski sixty years before thanks to Lisa Resch, who was nine years her elder. 'She was the ideal sportswoman. Her parents had money. Her father was a butcher and owned a shop. They had knives and forks to use when we went to dinner. My parents never did any sports.'

Kathe said that one of her team-mates, 'Guzzi' Lanschner, had worked with Leni Riefenstahl on her film of the 1936 Olympics in Berlin. It was a pity, I thought, that there wasn't a film of the Winter Olympics too. Oh, but there was. It used to be shown as a prelude to *Olympia*. It was only half an hour. Kathe herself appeared only briefly. Would I like to see it?

The 1936 Olympics sounded in some ways like the 1991 World Cup event: it was held in mid-February and there were lots of rowdy Canadians, a lone Australian and some Japanese competing. In those days the bob-sleigh track was improvised from slabs of ice carved out of the frozen lake.

Kathe's daughter drew the curtains. The film begins with a call to attention on the horn and the title – *Jungen Der Welt* (Youth of the World). The sound track is brassy and melodramatic. An aerial shot of a snowscape punctuated by two towns like sultanas poking through the icing on a cake gives way to an image of clouds forming and then blowing away. The mountain beneath shines out like a lighthouse.

In the opening ceremony it is still snowing. It only

starts snowing on that day, as if under orders. And it keeps on snowing to produce near-perfect conditions. Great thick scoops of snow plummet down. Olympic flags and swastikas flutter together from neighbouring poles. Adolf Hitler declares the Fourth Winter Olympics open and gives the Nazi salute. German athletes return the gesture with a rigid arm. The British team adopts the formal Olympic salute, with the right arm flung out like a Morris Minor indicator, the head swivelled to the left, but the crowd gives them an ovation anyway since one rigid arm is much like another.

Men march up and down on skis, then go cross-country with rifles slung on their backs. Every now and then they stop to take a shot at something. This is 'the military ski-patrol event,' Kathe tells me.

There is a blast of 'God Save the Queen'. Great Britain has taken bronze in the two-man bobsleigh. 'Look – that is the Bavarian bend! Everyone comes off here.'

Kathe was befriended by the British women and met Arnold Lunn who spoke excellent German. 'In those days you had to reckon with the English as opponents.'

In the stands the 'Father of Skiing', the first man in history to invent a discipline to be incorporated into the Olympic curriculum in his own lifetime, watched with mounting horror the games he called the 'Nazi Olympics'. He had repudiated calls for a boycott. To Lunn, the Olympics embodied the glory that was Greece, the ideals of chivalry, and the ethics of Christianity rolled into one. But Garmisch-Partenkirchen reminded him more of Sparta than of Athens. Though he was appointed referee of the slalom, he caused a scandal by refusing to take part in the opening procession or salute Hitler.

In the figure skating, a German pair is performing. 'They were Jews,' Kathe said. 'And they won! You can see how tense she is until she does that figure – and now she is all right. He was an architect: he used to plot all his moves on a board. I can't remember their names. I didn't really know them.'

Finally it is the turn of the *abfahrtslauf*, the downhill. There is some bumpy footage taken from the skier's point of view looking over the top of the skis. 'This is Hans Ertel – who did cross-country and ski-jump – he went with a camera strapped to his chest.'

A tangle of skiers, men and women, are careering down simultaneously. 'This wasn't in the race – why did they put it in? There – that is Christl!' Christl Cranz was Kathe's heroine. 'It was such a steep, steep hill. It's been cut too much – you don't see anyone cover the entire course.' For a second or two the camera holds on Kathe's face as she glides innocently by: she is without helmet or goggles and her unmasked features are set in rapt concentration; her long plaits flap up and down.

She wasn't thinking about prizes or sponsorship, there was no tour. 'It has changed a lot. There was a cable-car, but we had to walk a long way up to the start. There were still trees on the course then. You could go left or right – you had to have a feel for the country. You couldn't go straight as you can now. It was technically more difficult. The slalom was perfidious. I remember the Norwegians had better wax than we did and thermometers. Everybody waxed his own skis. We wore two pairs of socks and an anorak. The anorak was only invented in 1934. Anton Zeloss was a very good coach: he didn't explain, but he showed. 'Zeloss's combinations' he called them. We always had to take our shoulder with us around the curve. The old technique is coming back again.'

Kathe said that there were a lot of military personnel

at the Games, but they were mainly there 'to clear the course'. But wasn't there an element of propaganda in it, weren't the Germans trying to show what supreme human beings they were? 'It wasn't a big thing. If you look at what is happening now, we didn't make much out of it.'

She had a point. In the film, the ski-jump sequence was intercut with images of eagles wheeling through the clouds. Now Brian Stemmle wore an eagle emblazoned on his helmet. Nations and individuals played out their battles on the track or in the mountains. In 1936, surrounded by the apparatus of war, it was still possible to be carefree and lighthearted on skis.

'We used to do it just for fun,' Kathe said. 'We were not dedicated. It was natural to ski here. We didn't take much notice of the army and the flags. I didn't even understand what the Olympics were. I didn't realize my achievement.' In the combined downhill and slalom, Franz Pfnur of Germany won the Men's event and Christl Cranz the Ladies'. Kathe came second in the downhill in a time of five minutes eleven seconds. Peter Lunn, son of Arnold, finished twelfth out of sixty.

But sport was already a branch of politics. Hitler had plans for the Alpine skiers: they would be a symbol of purity and strength, moral pre-eminence and racial superiority. So he invited Kathe and Christl, the first German women to win Olympic medals, for dinner in Berlin at the Reichschancellery. Dinner with Hitler, just the three of them. I couldn't help wondering if Kathe and Christl were candidates for recruitment to his scheme for genetic engineering. I imagined silver candlesticks and white, white dinner plates and an inquisitorial doctor standing outside the door.

Kathe was embarrassed by her recollection. It was no longer possible for a German to remember meeting Hitler with equanimity. 'I was only eighteen. I didn't know what it was all about. I should have done, but I didn't. I don't like to talk about it now.' That was the virtue and the vice of dwelling in the mountain: being cut off from what was happening in the world below, like living on the moon in a bubble with an artificial atmosphere. The creature of the sky, like Baudelaire's albatross, might be crippled in falling to earth. Leaving Shangri-La the beautiful Lo-Tsen turns to dust and blows away. The Canadians never seemed to come down, it was too risky. Glenn said he wanted to go to Vienna – between Kitzbühel and Wengen – but it was too far from the mountains.

'After the war, all my good friends were dead or missing. It wasn't the same.' Kathe competed in one more FIS race in 1941 and then retired. Now she only paid nostalgic visits to the places she had once skied.

Kathe's Olympic silver medal (showing a three-horse chariot driven by a woman) and a certificate had been framed by her brother and were hanging on the wall in the living room next to one of her 1936 wooden skis, 2.05 metres long and made in Norway.

Lunn listened in disbelief to complacent after-dinner speeches which affirmed that 'the true League of Nations is the league of international sportsmen.' Skiing wasn't going to save the world. He regarded the Games as a rehearsal for Armageddon in which grim German efficiency overwhelmed happy-go-lucky British amateurism. 'The snows of Garmisch', he wrote, 'were flecked by the shadows of war.' One night he dreamed that England had been conquered in the year 2000 by Germany, which was in turn conquered by Japan five hundred years later, and that in the year AD *3036 he was standing by a river in Tokyo watching the recently revived Henley Regatta to the strains of a Japanese translation of the Eton Boating Song.*

18

NORWAY had more skiers in the top ten than any other nation. Their coach was the Austrian Dieter Bartsch, who was sacked by his own country and once coached the British team. Now he was sought after as an oracle and guru. I asked him what his secret was. 'Downhill is not just one event, it is many rolled into one. I train for the different skills – turning, jumping, speed – and then rely on the skiers themselves to put it all together.'

Downhill was all things to all men, it was the alpha and omega of the encyclopedia of winter games. 'It is a mosaic,' Patrick said. Every other event – slalom, speed skiing, ski-jump – was like a fraction of the whole, separated out and blown up out of proportion. They seemed to me like second-class substitutes for the real thing, but each of these disciplines had its own fanatical adherents and some claim to legitimacy. In Garmisch I had just missed a World Cup ski-jump contest. The 70-metre ramp was at the other end of town to the downhill.

Jorge Luis Borges wrote that 'fame is a form of incomprehension, perhaps the worst.' Michael Edwards took the same view. It was in 1988 at the Calgary Olympics that, as Eddie the Eagle, he conquered the world by coming last in the ski-jump. He was known far and wide for his pranks, his good humour in defeat, his never-say-die spirit, for strapping rockets to the underside of his skis. What he wanted to be known for was his skill and finesse and for winning something, anything.

Eddie hadn't done too well in the contest and he was sticking around to smooth out some bumps in his technique. He took me up the steps to the top of the jump. It was like climbing the Eiffel Tower. 'Want to give it a try?' he asked brightly.

The Canadians could have taken some good pictures here: it was like peering down into a 70-metre toilet bowl, an immense porcelain laundry chute. I couldn't get my breath and my eyes wouldn't focus.

'What got you into this?' I asked.

'I've always been a crazy bastard,' he said.

Eddie the Eagle came from a long line of crazy bastards. The ski-jump is not a modern stunt, but one of the primordial Nordic disciplines, dating back at least as far as the beginning of the eighteenth century. It was probably in 1840 that Sondre Norheim of Norway discovered that by landing on a downward slope he could safely jump further than any man before him. The Holmenkollen, embracing the Jump and the *langlauf*, was first held in Christiania (now Oslo) a hundred years ago and was, according to Lunn, 'the closest approximation in this degenerate age to the religious atmosphere of the classic Olympic Games.' The King of Norway, himself a keen jumper, presented the prizes. During the war dying men, broken under torture, scratched 'H' on their prison walls: the symbol of the Norwegian Resistance was the first letter of King Haakon's name and of the Holmenkollen. In 1950 the Oslo Ski Association organized a floodlit ski-jumping contest on Hampstead Heath. They trucked in a 60-foot tower of steel scaffolding, 45 tons of snow in insulated containers every day, and twenty-five leading jumpers. Fifty-two thousand spectators watched the final rounds of the 'London Challenge Cup'. The outrun was short, ending in a pile of hay, and jumpers were dug out with a pitchfork.

Eddie had a dream in which he is skiing down an almost vertical fall, skipping over rocks and swerving round trees. He is fast approaching the cliff edge, but he keeps on going, launching himself off into space, with the sea hundreds of feet below. Fortunately, he is wearing a parachute. He splashes down and swims confidently through shark-infested waters to his yacht where a beautiful woman awaits him.

He was the son of a Gloucestershire plasterer. An affinity with white walls ran in the family. To compensate for his myopia he wore thick lenses that misted up when he jumped. He didn't tan easily and he didn't wear the right clothes. He had a John Wayne jaw on a Stan Laurel face. People identified with him because he was an ordinary man with extraordinary ambitions. He may not have attained excellence, but he pursued it with a passion. He didn't win, but he showed medals weren't the only thing worth winning. Having begun jumping only eighteen months before the Olympics, it was a miracle that he was even taking part.

'I didn't come last,' he corrected me when we met up again at ground-level and holed up in a pizza parlour in town. 'Not all the time. I was fifty-eighth out of fifty-eight in the seventy-metre and fifty-fifth in the ninety.'

The media had made him famous, but they had also reduced him to a comic cut-out. He got fed up with the tag of gallant loser, court jester. Nobody took him seriously, but the truth was he was the most serious jumper there.

'I broke the British record at Calgary.' At first, no one was quite sure what the British record had been, or even if there was one. The Hampstead Heath record was 28 metres, but that was held by a Norwegian. Finally it came out that Guy Dixon had jumped one inch over 200 feet – 61 metres – on 24 February 1931 at Davos. British ski jumping had been officially discontinued in 1936. Eddie pushed the record up to 71 metres. Others tried to follow him, including one man who called himself 'Simon the Seagull'. But none stayed the course.

When the quiet and withdrawn fourteen year old first put on skis he found he could talk to girls and he became known as the 'kamikaze kid'. He started out as a downhiller. But there wasn't room for him in the team beside Boris and the Bell brothers. Jumping is one of the required skills in the downhill repertoire, so it was natural that he should take so readily to the ramps. After a few days of concussion and exaltation at Lake Placid in 1986, leapfrogging impatiently on to the loftiest platforms, he decided: 'This is what I was born for.'

Anyway, jumping was cheaper than downhill: you didn't need a lift-pass. Someone sold him the skis for $30 and he dug up some ancient jumping shoes for nothing, cracked and torn, from the bottom of a cupboard. One of them came apart when he was halfway down a 90-metre jump in Switzerland. There's no stopping, no turning round or second thoughts on a jump: once you start you're committed. Even if you have a heart seizure you've still got to jump.

When he crashed at Innsbruck in 1989 – 'it was ten past eleven in the morning and I was flying higher than ever before, and there was this cemetery at the bottom coming up to meet me and I panicked' – he smashed his collar bone, broke several ribs, cracked his skull, and damaged his kidneys. And still within three weeks he was jumping again.

His troubles weren't limited to injuries though. To some Eddie was the embodiment of Baron de Coubertin's Olympic ideal of struggle and participation; but to the bureaucrats and sponsors he was an anomaly, an aberration they could do without. Drambuie were pumping a small fortune into the Alpine team. Why should Eddie, who never received a penny in sponsorship – he scrubbed floors and washed dishes in ski resorts to pay for his flight to Calgary – and wasn't advertising anyone on his borrowed equipment and hand-me-down gear, steal the limelight? This was a man who had once bandaged up a broken jaw with a pillowcase and booked into a mental hospital when he couldn't afford a room for the night, a jumped-up ski bum, a screwball: what right had he to wear his country's colours?

On his triumphant return to England he recorded a song, 'Fly Eddie Fly', with an all-woman group 'The Eaglelettes'; Dustin Hoffman called from Hollywood wanting to make a film of his life. The British Ski Federation demanded their share of his earnings and insisted on him setting up a trust fund which would pay him just expenses if he wanted to carry on competing for Britain. Since 1988 Eddie had financed his skiing by opening supermarkets and golf clubs. He jumped over cars and buses for charity. And he bankrupted himself to the tune of £100,000 plus. It was enough to make anyone jump off a cliff.

The autobiography he published after the Olympics – *Eddie the Eagle: My Story* – wasn't the whole story. Now he wanted to write another more critical book that would 'blow the lid off skiing'. All he needed was a title and a writer. That and £20,000 in sponsorship just to keep going.

Now there was a rumour that the British Olympic Association was going to impose a new rule requiring all would-be Winter Olympic competitors to be in the top 50 per cent in their field. That would eliminate Eddie and, theoretically, most of the British team at a stroke. 'It's crazy,' Eddie said. 'If you applied that in tennis we'd have no one at Wimbledon. It's bureaucracy gone mad. We're going to have about a hundred people in Albertville – nine athletes and ninety officials.'

'It'll never happen,' Callahan said. 'He's your biggest asset. Even on Oahu people know his name. Most Hawaiians don't know the name of the President.'

Nine months later, the rule was brought in. The Eagle was out. We didn't have a ski-jump team anymore.

Sarah Lewis, manager of the British Alpine squad, said that the new regulations provided equal opportunity for all: 'It's not that Eddie's being excluded: he just doesn't qualify.'

The last time I saw Eddie he was back on the ramp still working on his technique. He was gathering speed as he approached the lip, holding his tuck, straining to keep those skis together and maintain his equilibrium against the forces that threatened to capsize him. When he took off he leaned into the updraft like the figurehead on a ship. I remembered his golden rule: 'The way in which you explode is the key.'

19

MAYBE what was keeping the Eagle down was not his technique but his equipment. 'He needs broad skis,' pronounced Callahan. Broader skis were the newest thing for longer flight. Eddie was strapped into a pair of toothpicks.

Speed skiing, held over a straight 'flying kilometre' course and contested by men in fibreglass souwesters and paper-thin rubber body-stockings going twice as fast as the fastest downhiller, was widely deemed to have boiled down to a battle between rival ski and aerodynamic clothing manufacturers. But even in the multi-faceted downhill the question of optimal equipment had become a collective obsession. The mountains were a laboratory in which ski companies tested out their technology to destruction. The downhill had become a race between competing guinea pigs.

That, at any rate, was Arnold Lunn's apocalyptic vision of the future. Transposing Spengler's doom-laden diagnosis in *Decline of the West* to skiing, he feared that 'downhill racing is approaching the final phase of the culture cycle, through which every great culture is doomed to pass, the creative spring-time, the summer of perfected achievement, the autumn still glorious with deciduous colouring, and the winter in which the frosts of scientific technique destroy the last flowering of inspiration.'

The first skis were simply slightly elongated snowshoes: planks of wood, staves of barrels that acquired a curl in the nose to hasten their passage through the snow (the Finno-Ugrian word *ski* means 'split wood', from the Indo-European root *skidh*, 'cleave', and is cognate with the Greek *schizo* and the Latin *scindo*). The Hoting ski dug up in Sweden and dating from 2500 BC was three feet eight inches long and four inches across. In the mid-nineteenth-century Sierra Nevada, John A. 'Snowshoe' Thomson made his own skis modelled on recollections of those he had seen as a boy in Norway. They were oak beams twelve feet long, four inches wide and weighed twenty-five pounds. They were held in place by a broad leather toe strap.

Almost any kind of wood would do, but hickory and ash were best. The smoother the finish the faster they went. Thomas à Becket's secretary wrote in 1180 that men with bones tied to their feet 'doe slide as swiftly as a birde flyeth in the aire'. The thirteenth-century *Könges-peilet*, or 'King's Mirror', a Norwegian treatise on court manners and northern phenomena, recounts that a wing-footed man

> can outstrip the swiftest hounds, or even the reindeer, which is itself twice as swift as the hart. For there are many men who are so swift upon their ski that they can strike down with the spear nine reindeer as they speed by in their course, and thereafter even more. This, indeed, is a thing which will seem marvellous, nay incredible and absurd, in all those lands where folk know not the art and cunning whereby boards can be trained to this great speed; who know not that on the mountains there is nothing among things which run upon the face

> of the earth which can escape the pursuit of that man who has boards beneath his feet, even though he be left no whit swifter than other men as soon as he has taken the boards from off his feet. But in other lands, where folk know not this art, no man will be found so swift but that he will lose all his swiftness as soon as these boards are bound to his feet.

Ultimately, it was speed itself that became the prey. In the twentieth century, trees and skeletons gave way to a sandwich of metal and plastic and fibreglass. Now the manufacturers were making constant technical refinements, mysteriously fine-tuning their designs, experimenting with new materials like cordon bleu cooks shuffling their ingredients, nuancing flex and rigidity, trimming the waist or fattening it, subtracting an ounce here, adding one there, and shaving precious fractions of seconds off potential times. But like Excalibur in the stone, the ultimate weapon is hard to dig out of the factory. Not all the men wearing Blizzard – or Atomic, or Rossignol – have an equal chance. The top skis went to the top skiers, the company flag carriers, so the fastest men would go even faster; conversely, the lower orders who never appeared on the podium were locked into a vicious circle of slow times and slower skis. When the Bells saw one of the top ten whistle by they would mutter, 'He has fast skis. *Very* fast skis.' Hans Anewanter said, 'You get into a spiral with skiing: the spiral can go up – or it can go down.'

But even if you are being showered with all the best skis, you still have to choose the right arrow from your quiver. It is only at the last moment that the ski rep makes his fateful decision, having reviewed the data on the course, checked air temperature and humidity, the size and texture of the snow crystals. When a race can be decided by hundredths of a second, victory hangs on masterminding the hardware. An infinitesimal error of judgement and you could blow the world title. The ski reps hated to share their theories and insights; one would hide his meticulously selected skis under his bed at night, fearful of spies or sabotage. Every year skis that were reputed to be outstandingly fast on certain surfaces would quietly disappear, swiped by rival manufacturers eager to crib their design.

There is no such thing as the perfect ski. The Parisian Jeannot Liard had been a shaper for Dynastar – who manufactured a million skis every year – all his working life. He described the ski as having a *taille de guêpe*, wasp-waisted and flaring out along each side in the arc of an imaginary circle. The curve corresponded to the kind of turn you wanted to make: in the case of slalom it was a small circle facilitating tight turns; the downhill circles, in contrast, had a much wider radius with a flatter circumference implying a straighter, more flowing run with broader, sweeping ellipses through the snow. The geometry of your trajectory down the mountain was always already prefigured in the form of the ski. To the factories the skiers were just passengers on board vehicles that did all the steering themselves. '*Il faut d'abord avoir le bon cheval,*' said Jeannot. '*Un bon descendeur.*'

There was a science to downhill but there was always room for human error. Konrad Bartelski was Britain's top skier in the seventies and early eighties, but he was famous for his spectacular falls. He used to test out his equipment and his posture in a windtunnel in Nuneaton. The engineers boasted of being able to simulate just about everything: the exact conditions for trucks, racing cars, aeroplanes, and the turbulent forces that pluck at a skier's body at high speed. When Bartelski fell on a tree stump in Val Gardena in 1982 they sent him a telegram saying: 'Sorry unable to simulate tree stumps. Get well soon.'

Surfers wax their boards to provide a waterproof grip for their feet; skiers wax their skis, in contrast, to make them more slippery and increase their speed over the snow. Norsemen of old used to smear pig's fat over their reindeer bones. Downhillers swore by their waxes, whose composition was a deadly secret. The idea of borrowing someone's wax was as unthinkable as asking a footballer for his boots.

In 1984 the Italians came up with a formula that made them virtually invincible, like Asterix's magic potion. One dark night the disgruntled keeper of the wax passed a sample to an Austrian spy who promised him riches and a better job. The Austrians duly prospered and garnered medals in the Olympic downhill, spurning the luckless traitor who had been sacked by the Italians.

Bertrand was the French wax man. I met him once in the windowless cellar where he worked. You never saw him out on the slopes. His senses were so finely tuned that too much raw experience would have sent him spinning into overload. There was a dim light in his den, but he didn't really need it: like a connoisseur of fine wines, he could tell waxes apart by their bouquet alone. His old chiselled nose twitched like a mole's. For a second opinion he would sometimes resort to his palate and roll a ball of wax around his tongue. *Ça sent bon* or *bonne saveur* were his highest accolades. He concocted mixtures of paraffin, graphite and silicon in silver cauldrons like an alchemist. To some all waxes were alike, but to Bertrand every wax had its own individual and complex personality, a particular synthesis of perfume, density, granulosity. 'The more you reduce friction, the faster you slide,' he explained. '*Mais attention*! The ski can be too smooth, like car tyres; you have to have resistance as well as flow. My job is never finished.'

There was a mystique attached to the length of your skis. Short skis, not much longer than your foot, were strictly for beginners. The downhill men went as long as 2.30 metres. The longer your skis the faster you skied. That was the theory anyway. Travelling light, I was at the mercy of the skis I hired. At times I had wings on my feet, at others matching tombstones. Callahan advised me to stick with 1.95s: 'They're a good compromise: you won't break any records in them, but you won't break any bones either.'

In Garmisch there was a section of the mountain known as Hell. When I'd clawed my way up out of the underworld, white-sheeted like a ghost, I limped back to the ski-hire shop, dragging my skis behind me like a cross.

'So, you like the two metres then?' The beefy, bearded man behind the counter extended a hearty welcome.

'But I said 1.95s.'

'No 1.95s left. I give you two metres instead. Better, no?'

'No,' I said. Five centimetres was the difference between joy and despair, heaven and hell.

But even when I was safely back on 1.95s, I was still going astray on deep snow. It was Callahan who came up with the answer. 'Why don't you try a snowboard?' he said. 'The ultimate powder vehicle. Only one edge to worry about and no poles.' The trouble with two skis was getting them to do the same thing at the same time. I was riding schizoid skis, Dr Jekyll on one foot and Mr Hyde on the other, and they were ripping me apart. A snowboard, a single surface accommodating both feet, a surfboard adapted to crystallized waves, would instantly heal this split personality.

Snowboards were a recent invention but there were already snowboarding contests. In some parts of the world there are even combined surfing and snowboarding events: you catch a wave on the Californian coast or in Biarritz, then drive up into the Sierra Nevada or the Pyrenees and slide down another kind of face. Ted Deerhurst had been on the pro surfing tour for over a decade without ever winning a contest; but he could ski and so when the first OP Wintersurf Pro took place at Huntington Beach and Big Bear Mountain he felt this was a heaven-sent opportunity to change his luck. 'I hadn't really mastered the snowboard,' he explained to me one day. 'But I thought to myself, "What the hell – it's only skiing, at least you can't drown up here." Then I fell six hundred feet.' He spent the next year in a wheelchair. I got away with severe bruising and abrasions.

To Patrick, snowboards and monoskis were just a fashion that would melt away. 'How many feet do you have?' he would say. He was apt to quote the wise words of Franz Klammer, the Austrian who won a record twenty-five World Cup victories in the seventies: 'I ski against myself and no one else. And I know that if I beat myself then no one can beat me.'

Elja also thought my problems were psychological. In the Garmisch press centre canteen she ushered me over

20

ALBERTO Tomba had won another slalom and had edged past Heinzer in the overall World Cup rankings. Thusfar the title looked like being a straight battle between downhill and slalom. But coming up behind and threatening to overhaul the two main contenders – Heinzer the thesis and Tomba the antithesis – was a third force, a synthesis, embracing the opposite ends of the Alpine spectrum: Marc Girardelli.

I thought of Girardelli as a gifted and erratic downhiller, but in fact he was one of that rare breed of all-rounders who also took time off to boogie around poles. He was an Austrian with Italian blood and French equipment who skied for Luxembourg. He *was* the Luxembourg team; it was a flag of convenience. There was controversy over why he didn't ski for Austria. Girardelli said it was because the Austrian Ski Federation rejected him as a kid so he broke away determined to prove himself. The Austrians said it was because he was too much of a solo operator to fit into a team.

He was twenty-seven and had won the overall World Cup title three times, a record bettered only by Stenmark and Zurbriggen. At Val d'Isère he was the man everyone wanted to see; Sergio Tacchini had chosen him to succeed Zurbriggen as the figurehead of their multi-million promotional campaign. But he finished fifty-ninth out of sixty, five seconds adrift of Leonhard Stock and behind even the Brits. It was his first downhill since a bad smash two years before. He was reckoned to be in decline, barely recovered from injury, and psyched out by his accident. He could still slalom (fourth place at Sestrière behind Tomba in December), but he couldn't downhill any more. He had lost his nerve and couldn't handle speed. At Val Gardena he started among the top fifteen seeds, but he finished with the pack. It was an embarrassment. The high mountain and the dark canyon of downhill were no place for a wounded man to hide. There was no escape from the glare of the sun and the cruel objectivity of the clock.

Off the course, Girardelli was a recluse. He hardly ever gave interviews to the press. I wasn't even sure what he looked like. Zipped-up, helmeted, and masked like a bank robber, he might as well have been the Invisible Man swathed in bandages for all I saw of him as he sped by. He vanished suddenly after his races; when I went to his hotel, it was the wrong hotel, or he was out. Elja told me that he was an astronomer in his spare time, who spoke numerous languages and read Macchiavelli and Umberto Eco.

It was in Garmisch that I came up against Helmut Girardelli. Helmut was more than Marc's father, he was his trainer and manager, his greatest supporter and his sternest critic. He was a large cantankerous man who watched over his son and was quick to upbraid members of rival teams when they looked like squeezing him out. But he was even-handed: Marc got plenty of flak when he lost. When *they* lost it would be truer to say. Helmut felt just as bad as his son about finishing at the back of the field, as if he were still smarting over the Austrian slight. Now he was gloomily examining the dregs of a mighty mug of German beer.

'Marc does not want to be known as another Stenmark,' he said. In the seventies and eighties Sweden's Ingemar Stenmark had accumulated the greatest number of World Cup points of any competitor before or since, together with five Olympic gold medals. He was a perfectionist who left nothing to chance. He had determination, strength and balance. What he lacked was courage: he flatly refused to go fast and wouldn't touch downhill. Stenmark was the Tomba of his day.

'In the slalom, Marc is good,' Helmut said. 'But he has lost his feel for downhill. He just goes to it like he is going to work. And if you race a downhill like it is work, then what you do is not downhill. It needs more.'

Brian James of *The Times*, a heavily built and unathletic man who could move fast when he needed to, claimed an exclusive with Girardelli when he managed to exchange a few words with him as the racer strode grim-faced through a ruck of men celebrating times several seconds faster than his own. I bought him a sandwich and pumped him for details.

Brian said: 'I asked him, "What ails? Is it physical or mental?"'

'And what did he say?'

'He said, "I don't know. Ask me at the end of the season." And he laughed a mirthless laugh.'

Skiers split into two groups in their attitude towards being interviewed. On the one hand, there were those like Girardelli who were a source of perpetual fascination to the press and therefore played hard to get, or because they were elusive or inaccessible became fascinating; on the other hand, there were those, generally less successful, whose names rarely appeared in the press, except at the bottom of the page in very small print, and who were desperate to be taken seriously and given attention proportionate to their ambitions.

While I was out looking for Girardelli I kept running into Boris and the Bells. One day Denis O'Brien said to me, 'Please give my sponsors a mention. They'd be so chuffed.' Different bits of him were sponsored by Raichle, Blizzard, Salomon, and Madigans Entertainment Group.

Similarly, I was beginning to see, the downhill racer was a composite creature: it was difficult to hang a single label on him. 'What makes the true downhiller then?' I asked Elja.

'The downhiller is like Hamlet: everyone and no one,' she said.

The downhill wasn't just for a hardcore band of daredevils and kamikaze cases, all balls and no brain, publicity seekers and fortune hunters; it was for saints and engineers, milkmaids and absent-minded professors, crazy Canucks and rogue Ozzies, extroverts and invisible men. For some downhill was paradise; for others purgatory. It was two minutes in which you tasted eternity, as compressed as the Bible on the back of a postage stamp, a brutal encounter with physical reality which imparted a dreamlike sense of transcendence. The mountains were a magnifying glass which heightened and distorted the make-up of the individual and a prism which split the one into the many. I wasn't the only one looking for some kind of truth; maybe all skiers were.

Elja authorized me to quote from her dreams and gave me complete *carte blanche*. 'Write anything you like,' she said. 'I understand that what you put on the page can't possibly be *me*. I am only your projection.' She assumed that anything I wrote would be fiction. Anything anyone wrote was fiction. Literature was just writing down your dreams. In fact, there were a few scattered poems mixed up in her dream-file. They were, on the whole, less well-balanced than her dreams. 'Make sure you put me in some steamy sex scenes,' she said. It was like being asked to mention her sponsors. She believed that dreams fulfilled a compensatory function for most people: what you couldn't pull off during the day you were a natural at during the night. Writing, she supposed, was the same: it was my job to rectify reality in accordance with her desires. '*You are the Alchemist,*' she said.

It wasn't easy to find love on the tour. Ten years ago Elja had joined a computer dating agency and had been fixed up with a string of unsuited suitors, from the wrong town or the wrong background, too old, too young, too rich, too poor, bricklayers, sailors, accountants, a psychiatric nurse who took her to an ice-rink, men who just wanted to have sex with her, men who didn't want to have sex with her, and one guy who said he was going to ask for his money back. 'It wasn't anything personal,' she said.

She recalled a garage mechanic who sat there shaking all the while they were together. His previous wife had tried to murder him and had been locked up. One man, who produced 3-D computerized ads for television, had been hospitalized twice for psychosis. He thought he was a white witch whose mission in life was to seek out and destroy black witches. He carried a fly spray around with him and zapped passing insects in the belief that they were 'agents of darkness'. He wouldn't eat in restaurants for fear that the cooks had poisoned the meat. He was on drugs for manic depression. 'He was a nice guy – warm and sensitive. Not relationship material though.' She always looked for the positive elements in her dates.

Self-expression was Elja's first commandment. Cosimo didn't want me to write about him at all. 'Leave me out,' he growled. 'Make me unrecognizable.'

Recording what Cosimo said was like tapping his telephone, a betrayal of trust. 'Don't quote me, don't use my name. You'll lose a friend,' he said. He was like some technological primitive afraid that photography would rob him of his soul. The trouble with journalism was that it sliced reality up into pieces, pars and headlines. And Cosimo didn't want to be squashed to fit. 'I would never consent to be interviewed,' he said. 'It is like rape, a violation.'

Cosimo wanted the whole truth and nothing but the truth. And unless truth were whole, unless it included everything and left nothing out, then it would be false. The only representation of Cosimo that he trusted was himself.

'Truth is collective and social not private,' he decreed. Even though Cosimo was a criminologist, he wasn't interested in particular crimes and criminals and famous cases. He specialized in global networks and whole populations; the human condition at large, not this or that human; Man not men and women; groups, tribes, cultures; the destiny of mankind. He wanted to get at the Form or Idea behind appearances, the Grand Theory that would account for all manifestations of a phenomenon. Since everything connected up with everything else in a single gigantic totality, nothing less than embracing the entire universe would really do. What he was after was more the criminological equivalent of $e = mc^2$ than the solution to the mystery of the Sign of Four.

This attitude of his (I theorized) explained why he liked mountains so much – because they offered an Olympian perspective on the world below; either that or his passion for mountains generated his propensity for taking the broad view. When he went up into the mountains, it was as if he were temporarily bidding farewell to all that, rising above the mêlée of everyday illusions and ascending to the realm of true philosophy.

The concept of the General Will wouldn't have made much sense to Callahan. To his way of thinking, there were nothing but individuals in the world. Only moments were meaningful, eternity didn't exist. There was no pattern to life, history was pure contingency, a succession of chance happenings, an accumulation of atoms, a string of exclamation marks devoid of syntax. Everything was snapshots: if you were in the right place at the right time you could enjoy instantaneous flashes of experience. Behind the neon-lit façades of existence, there was nothing but darkness. Appearances *were* reality.

While Cosimo was content with *being* in the mountains, Callahan was never at ease unless he was *doing*. He had the hunted air of a man on the run, a fugitive from justice who couldn't afford to stay long in any one place in case he was traced, apprehended and put away.

Cosimo feared I would be incapable of telling the truth in all its complexity; Callahan feared I was incapable of lying enough to save his skin. 'Put that notebook away,' he would say as he filled me in on the latest scandal. 'Don't quote me – or I'm history.' He was jumpy about his girlfriend and how she'd react if she ever read the truth instead of his seemingly innocent postcards back home. 'I'm taking the Fifth Amendment,' he said. 'I don't want to incriminate myself.'

For Callahan, propositions were picture postcards of reality that could be sent around the world, locating him in time and space and giving away his whereabouts to all his enemies and lovers. But as much as he dreaded exposure he also craved it. Secretly, he wanted to be recognized. 'This *wahine* comes up to me the other day,' he told me. 'She'd read something you'd written about me. "I never knew you were such a bastard," she said. Now everyone knows.'

While some people acted up for his camera, Callahan acted up for my pen. I sometimes had the impression he was giving me quotes. There were times he would behave badly just to provide colourful material. 'Hey, Andy, write this down, will you. "Callahan had a dick that, fully extended, was well over a foot long. He had the biggest dong in the world. It was a 1000 mm monster." That ought to get a good response.'

21

I HAD spent the winter going up and down mountains like a window cleaner on his ladder. It was only natural that when I wanted a break between Garmisch and Kitzbühel I should go skiing. I had agreed to join up with Heather and her family in the Pyrenees. Callahan was scoping Supertubes in Portugal.

Cauterets was three hours south-west of Toulouse and a thousand or so metres up. It was a spa in summer with therapy for arthritis and rheumatism. In winter it drummed up business for later in the year by putting people on skis.

Elja told me that Girardelli's secret fear was being overtaken by younger men. Mine was being overtaken by my own son. At birth he weighed in at a mighty 9 lbs 3 oz and had already outgrown his first set of clothes. He was a colossus who could drink me under the table and acquired extra poundage even as he slept. I was trying to put on weight too, just to stay ahead, but no matter what I did I still had the feeling he was gaining on me. It was probably just as well he was too young to go up in the cable-car and had to stay in town with his mother.

But there was no escaping George. George was Australian, Heather's blond twelve-year-old half-brother. He had been brought up in Perth, on the west coast, thousands of miles from the nearest mountain. And yet here he was skiing like Steve Lee. Steve Lee was his hero. George was a reckless daredevil who lived for excitement and danger. Extreme was his favourite word. Another of his heroes was John Falkiner, an Australian stuntman who lived in Verbier, doubled for 007, and had broken most of the bones in his body, some several times over. George showed me a photograph of him skiing out of a helicopter into blue space.

George had been in Cauterets before. He knew the mountain well and offered his services as guide and mentor. He regaled me with the story of three people who had died the previous week, a man, a woman and their son. He took me up to the icy pinnacle they had pushed off from. We edged out on to a parapet and he pointed down to the shadowy abyss below. It was the off-piste side of the mountain, with a sheer take-off of pure ice – so steep the snow couldn't hold – and no way back, a corridor, then a lot of nothing with mist hanging over it. 'That's where they went,' he said. Above us was a grey crag with a vertical drop of 250 metres. 'It must have been like falling off that,' he said, jabbing his thumb up. '*Le grand trou* they call it.' There was a triangular warning sign punched into the mountainside: *Vous entrez ce zone sous votre responsabilité*. It was a red rag to George. He thrust at it with his pole as he passed.

In the early days, all skiing was *ski extrême*. It was a handful of fanatics plotting new routes through unknown territory. There was a time when another set of ski tracks on your path would occasion as much astonishment as the footprints of the yeti. But vast tracts of the Alps were quickly domesticated and tamed. By the middle of the twentieth century all the skiable terrain had been skied. It only remained to ski the to her table and insisted on buying me a coffee. 'Have you tried inner skiing?' she asked. I had to visualize before I could actualize. Skiing was above all a mental exercise, physical reality was incidental. The reason people failed to be good skiers was because they saw themselves as failures. She said that she only had to speak to someone for half an hour to predict how they'd ski. Conversely, she could read a set of tracks in the snow like a palmist tracing lifelines in the hand.

Elja was a student of polarity therapy and was thinking about taking it up as a career. She told me that there were plus and minus poles at either end of the body, in the head and the feet, with neutral somewhere in-between. The point of the therapy was to release blockages of energy and this was to be achieved by connecting up the opposite ends of the self.

She'd just returned from a course. 'One man there was amazing – he connected up his thigh with his jaw straight away.'

'I've done that a few times,' I said.

unskiable. Extreme skiing in its modern manifestation arose out of the sense that mainstream skiing was hedged in by rules and regulations, seatbelts and crash helmets, and that life in general was too safe and settled. Extreme skiing begins at the point where if you fall, you die.

The first ascents of most mountains were by now passing into history and legend. It was 200 years since Mont Blanc was conquered. But in the 1960s the first *descents* had still barely been contemplated. The early pioneers were extreme climbers who were looking to get back down again with interest. Conventional thinking held that the needle-like peaks, glaciers, and gullies around Chamonix in the Massif du Mont Blanc could only be cautiously traversed with the aid of ropes, crampons, and ice-axes. They took calculated risks, painstakingly mapping out their routes down on the way up. But one slip of an edge could send the skier plummeting thousands of feet. It was the ultimate downhill, without clocks and timekeepers, gates and magic wands.

The breakthrough came in 1967 when Sylvain Saudan, a Swiss mountain guide, skied the Spenser Couloir, a fifty-degree climb, and earned himself the title, *Skieur de l'Impossible.* Before people said he was crazy. After they said he was crazy and lucky. But then he repeated the feat three or four times over. You can't be lucky every time. Saudan progressed to the northeast face of the Eiger and the southwest face of McKinley, an itinerary that culminated in 1982 with the first ski descent of Pakistan's 8000 metre Hidden Peak. He set up a helicopter skiing business in Kashmir with the assistance of the Indian army, but was grounded by civil war.

But when Iraq set fire to the oilwells of Kuwait, the snow in the Himalayas turned black. Now Saudan gave lectures to the employees of IBM and Caterpillar on fostering motivation and developing a 'winning attitude'.

Patrick Vallençant was a bearded iconoclast who dressed in pink from head to toe and subverted Alpine traditions by bragging, publicity-seeking, and making money. He sneered at the hallowed establishment of the Compagnie des Guides de Chamonix and set up his own rival school. His notoriety hung on opening up descents steeper than had ever been imagined. Weaving beneath the wires of the world's most vertiginous cable-car run, he skied the north face of the Aiguille du Midi, a column of ice that pokes up out of the Alps like a space rocket. This was the first time any skier had approached a drop of sixty degrees. Now Vallençant was dead, killed during a routine rock climb, the equivalent for an extremist of crossing the road. His wife died a year later diving off a crane, her leg tied to an elasticated rope.

The progenitor of the third generation was Jean-Marc Boivin, the son of a mathematics professor from Dijon, who began by humping equipment for Vallençant's film crews. In 1986 he was elected Maître des Quatre Faces for climbing alone and unroped four of the most formidable north faces in the world – the Aiguille Verte, the Droites, the Courtes and the Grandes Jorasses – all in a single day. On 17 April 1987 he was dropped by helicopter on the summit of the Dru, a three-and-a-half-thousand-metre granite monolith. His goal was the first descent of the South Couloir, a sheer snow gully that ends abruptly in an overhanging ice cliff.

The original Norwegians langlaufed over terrain flat to

bumpy. Lunn maintained that the fun only began at thirty degrees. The blackest of black slopes pushed the angle up to forty. The South Couloir exceeded sixty degrees. This was not just a steeper slope than all previous extreme descents, but broken, disconnected by bands of rock. Climbers have fallen over 400 metres down snow gullies and lived, but no one could survive a fall from the Dru. Boivin calmly skied to the edge of the cliff, uncoiled a rope and abseiled down to the slopes below.

In 1988 he set an unbreakable record for the highest launch of a paraglider by taking off from the summit of Everest. Having reached the grand old age of thirty-nine, thereby attaining a reputation for immortality among his fellows, he died in the steaming jungles of Venezuela, trying to parachute from Angel Falls, the tallest waterfall in the world.

American extremists wore day-glo mohican haircuts and leather jackets and tossed themselves off cliffs like cartoon characters who could never die. Videos of their exploits had been outlawed as a bad influence on the young.

It was too late for George: he was already having a bad influence on me. Back in town we lingered in front of a series of photographs in a shop window. They showed a family on skis, then just the top of their heads, and then the people dropped out of the frame and there was nothing left but sky. They had been taken on the summit by a local photographer who had backed up to try and get the large group in his sights. He had stepped over the edge backwards and, like a true professional, kept his finger on the button as he fell.

George was in love with the idea of sudden violent death. Dying was a good sign that you had been living intensely. If you were still alive by the time you reached my age then you weren't really trying. As if he were reading from the Bible, he quoted the words of Bruno Gouvy, who had invented sky-surfing and died snow-boarding the Aiguille Verte: 'There is a chance I might be killed. But in exchange, I have such a powerful sense of being alive. It's a bargain. I look at the risk, I take every step to minimize it, and in exchange for this little risk, I receive such a huge joy in living. Without risk, the sun is just the sun, grass is just grass. With risk, common things have incredible freshness.'

George told me riddles whose common denominator was dead bodies, usually lots of them.

> There's a cabin on the side of the mountain with two dead men inside it. They're wearing parachutes. Question: how did they die? Answer: in a plane crash – the cabin is an aeroplane cabin.
>
> A man turns the light out and commits suicide. In the morning there are hundreds of dead bodies on the ground outside his house. Question: who was he? Answer: the lighthouse keeper.

Fatal accidents and self-destruction, cannibalism and ritual murder, were meat and drink to this boy, but he was particularly fond of the idea of falling to your death from a great height. It seemed like a kind of ambition in him and enabled him to ski faster than anyone else. But he worried about me and looked over his shoulder from time to time to see if I was still there. Once he picked me out of a giant mogul like a solicitous St Bernard. 'Are you all right, Andy?' he said, wiping snow from my face.

'What you need is the Rossignol 7SK's, they'll give you better edge hold.'

George knew the age of the Pyrenees and said they were 'young' mountains by comparison with the Alps. 'See – they have a browny, crumbly texture, not smooth, black rock.' It was as if he'd been around when they were born. 'It's odd to think there were no mountains once – it was a real flat earth.' When I was twelve, all I had seen was Essex, so I thought the earth was flat and if you went too far you would drop off the edge. I still thought that last part.

On the Saturday of that week, George and his younger sister Sophie were competing in a race for under-fourteens. I had to cover the downhill in Kitzbühel on the same day, so I missed it, but I heard later what had happened. George was favourite to win. The weather was bad, the clouds were low, and visibility was virtually nil. You could barely see your own poles. It should have been called off. George's father took him on one side and counselled him to take it easy, the way he always did. George wasn't listening. What did his father know about these things? If you wanted to win you went in a straight line as fast as you could go. Everything else was just hooey.

They were sent off in pairs and George went with Sophie. She had a stronger instinct for self-preservation and skied in tight, cautious arcs. Her instructor told her, '*Il faut se dynamiser un peu.*' No one ever told George to 'dynamize' himself: it would have been like telling a hurricane to blow harder. George had a word for it: 'hooning'. 'He's really hooning,' he would say as one of the hard men shot by. George hooned from the start line and disappeared into the mist.

He came last. He took a wrong turn, lost his way, and had to trek back to the finish. That night he was moody and sardonic, cursing his luck and the organizers who had unexpectedly altered the route of the course. He refused to go to the awards party. Gérard, his instructor, came to the Hotel de Paris and pinned on his *troisième étoile* and said, 'You're not a student any more. Now you have the right to go anywhere on the mountain.'

Still George was depressed. Heather tried to console him. 'You can cope,' she said.

He put all his bitterness and rage into his reply. 'Can I?' he said.

22

THERE was a story about Glen Plake, the American extremist with the foot-high mohican. Someone asked him, if he were to be reincarnated as an animal, what kind of animal would he like to be? He thought about it for a while and then replied, 'Me.'

When I went to see Pierre Tardivel, the last of the third generation of French extremists, who skied down stalagmites of ice for a living, I was half expecting to meet a wild man, a maniac, a zany, egocentric lunatic with a deathwish, *le skieur fou* as one newspaper had dubbed him. I couldn't have been more wrong. He lived down the street from the casino in Annecy, a few hillsides along the valley from Mont Blanc. That was the closest he got to gambling.

He took me for a drive round the beautiful lake that Lamartine had once apostrophized and likened to a mirror and memory bank of fugitive human passions. It was like circling the bottom of a crystal bowl. All about us rose the dreaming spires of the Aiguilles. By chance my visit coincided with a ballooning event, a *montgolfiade*, and iridescent bubbles, a Zeppelin, and a ten-thousand-litre bottle of Orangina were climbing up the mountainside. One or two of the *montgolfières* were already falling back to earth in slow-motion, skipping over the trees, their burners still winking occasionally. 'What goes up must come down,' Pierre said. 'And vice versa.' That was his guiding principle in life.

A thousand metres above us a speck of a man was clinging from a crumbly vertical, with acres of sheer rock all round him. 'This is natural here,' Pierre said, 'like breathing.' There was no point asking him why he did what he did: he thought everyone was doing it. He couldn't envisage living any other way. His name meant stone or rock. Jean-Paul Sartre used a *pierre* as his symbol of the *en-soi,* the untroubled, unselfconscious material world; the *pour-soi,* the self-reflecting consciousness, that was also *en-soi,* the impossible *pour-soi-en-soi,* was his paradoxical definition of God.

Pierre had tousled corn-gold hair, narrow green eyes, and the physique of a long-distance runner. It was a frustrating time for him. He was waiting to do a *première* down the Italian side of Mont Blanc, but the conditions weren't right. The sky was clear, but the temperature was too high and there was a risk of avalanche. 'It's soup,' he said bitterly as he put down the phone after speaking to the *météo* for the tenth time. Sometimes it was too cold and the skis wouldn't grip. If the snow was not dense enough the edges would cut straight through it and hit ice. There was only a small window of opportunity for the extremist and it was getting smaller all the time. You used to be able to ski the high mountains right through summer; twenty years ago Saudan had skied the Spenser as late as October. Now the limit of the serious season was more like May to June. It was only possible to ski sixty degrees-plus two or three times a year. Glen Plake and the Americans were in Chamonix, but Pierre wasn't impressed. 'It is too early,' he said. 'Now they can only ski the easy couloirs, the south faces.' He pointed up into the mountains. 'Look, the really interesting ones – *les trucs sévères* – are black where the wind has blown the snow off.' June, when the rain fell as snow high up, would be best for the *faces nords*. 'I'd rather wait for the snow.'

We had dinner outside on the shore of the lake. It was almost sultry in the spring sun and wisteria was already blooming on the walls. Pierre laughed at the idea of a training diet and ate everything, knowing he would burn it off the next time he went running up a mountain with a boulder in his backpack. Pierre Tardivel was a scholar of skiing, a professor of snow sciences. He had done years of research and his knowledge of his subject was watertight. He didn't start skiing until he was thirteen. He built up to it progressively, gradually accumulating the know-how he would need later – first rock climbing, next alpinism, and only then turning to new ways of getting down the faces he had climbed. He was only seventeen or eighteen when he clocked up his first firsts – the Y Couloir at Argentière, the East Side of the Col du Diable. Now, on short sections, he had hit the limit of 70 degrees; beyond that snow wouldn't cling to the rock. The key was understanding the snow: a 50-degree slope with ice was more difficult than 60 degrees with good snow. At every turn the question Pierre asked himself was, '*Comment est la neige*?', gauging colour, granulosity, compactness.

This is where Gouvy went wrong on the Aiguille Verte. 'He took the helicopter up. So he didn't know what he would meet coming down. That was a great error. He never saw the black ice, it was under a thin layer of powder.' Pierre didn't approve of Boivin's crazy stunts either. 'It is necessary to be serious, to be reasonable in one's madness.' The fashion for *enchaînements*, the back-to-back linked climbs and descents, he rejected as 'a cross between triathlon and Russian roulette.' He didn't like to take stupid risks. He knew he would only ever make one mistake. He used to be a teller in a bank before he went full-time in 1988 and he still insisted on totting up and calculating his chances to several decimal places. 'I don't like the word extreme,' he said. 'What I do is never extreme. If I'm not a hundred per cent certain I don't go.' It was the rest of us who were extreme.

Usually you had to start the climb at first light, or in darkness, to be ready to descend when it was still early and the snow remained cold. Much later and it would be impossible. The most dangerous part of any descent is the start. The muscles you use for coming down are different to the ones you use for going up. And the muscles you haven't used are cold, almost numb. But there's no way you can start gradually and warm up; you have to kick-start. For the Face Nord des Courtes it was three or four hours up; only one hour down – or eternity. At this degree of declivity, every turn is essentially a jump: take-off, trajectory, and landing. Kick hard with the uphill ski, spin round, skid and carve with the edge again.

There used to be a healthy rivalry between the French extremists: they would be secretive about their plans, then every so often they would run into one another on the same summit. 'You, here! But you said you were doing the Pyramide today.' 'I thought you were supposed to be on the Dolent.' And they would laugh and ski down together.

But now Pierre had no rivals, there was no one left to ski with. He was the last extreme skier. Extreme skiing was not only running out of skiers in Europe, it was running out of skiing. Ten years before there were still many untouched couloirs; now they bore the scars of innumerable descents. Extraordinary exploits had become ordinary, banal. Fifty to fifty-five degrees was now merely for training, almost a nursery slope. To someone like Tardivel there was really only one challenge left: the Himalayas and Everest. 'Everest,' Pierre rolled the word around his mouth. 'That makes you dream, no?'

Since Hillary it had been climbed thousands of times; on one day in March alone there were twenty-nine ascents. But for the downhill skier it was still virgin territory. 'Technically, Everest is not difficult – no more difficult than, say, Mont Blanc. The problem is one of immensity, of scale, you must multiply time and effort many times. The cold is more intense, the avalanches are heavier, the distances are enormous. Coming down should be easy, it is getting up to the start that is hard.'

Pierre was planning an expedition in the summer that would make him the first man to ski Everest from top to bottom. In 1970 Yuichiro Miura had skied from Camp Four, 8000 metres high, only 800 metres from the summit. The Japanese caravan was in the grand tradition of the heavy expedition. Eight hundred porters carried 25 tons of material. Miura was attended not just by a doctor and a dentist but a hairdresser as well. To stay in shape before the descent he had brought along dumbells, weights and a practise-your-turn machine. He didn't really need the turning machine, he was planning to take it straight, as if it were the Flying Kilometre he had once competed in at Cervinia.

A cave-in claimed a half-dozen sherpas, but it was a point of honour for both the Japanese and the Tibetans not to give up. Miura quoted Miyamoto Musashi, a seventeenth-century Japanese swordsman and poet: 'The way of the samurai is the resolute acceptance of death.' By the time they reached Col Sud, the team had diminished from the original 800 to eight. Before making his attempt, Miura built a stone cairn on the mountain-side and placed his shaving mirror on it, saying that it was a 'symbol of the human soul'. He was trying to humanize the mountain by sending back to it the reflection of its own image. What made the mountain so strong and unforgiving was that, unlike the human, it had no self-consciousness: it was undiluted *en-soi*. Perhaps Miura conjectured that a self-conscious mountain, an *en-soi-pour-soi*, would be a more equal adversary.

The slope down to the Western Cwm is so steep that no climber has attempted it before. After six seconds Miura is travelling over the wind-rippled surface at 160 km per hour on his 2.40 m skis. He pulls the rip cord that will open his parachute – tested on the heights of Mount Fuji – and the parachute opens, but the air is too thin at this altitude for it to have any braking effect and he continues to gain speed. He now has no option but to try turning, but his edges can find no hold on the ice. After two minutes and several kilometres of the purest downhill ever skied, Miura falls. That is to say, he is already falling but now he has lost a ski and is continuing his fall on his back, still holding on to both poles, and tumbling irreversibly out of control over a stubble of rocks. The rocks slow him, but still he falls, digging hands, elbows, feet, into the unyielding surface. When he stops a few yards short of a crevasse, he is inert, his ribs smashed, but alive.

'Who can say if his attempt was a success or a failure?' said Pierre.

He took me back to his apartment. There were two books by Frank Slaughter on his shelves: *Afin que nul ne meure* and *Non pas la mort mais l'amour*. Pierre showed me the skis he kept on top of his wardrobe at the back. 'I don't have cause to use them very often,' he said. They were his Everest skis: Dynastar 'Extreme Vertical'. The main problem in tackling Everest was weight. Jeannot Liard worked for a month making a prototype and stripping it down, eliminating everything but the indispensable. The Extreme Verticals were only 1.80 m long and weighed 1.8 kg each, barely more than half the weight of the factory model. They had no top edge or aluminium badge in the toe, but were rigid and strong: no one wants to snap a ski half way down Everest. Pierre made his own bindings with both fixed and Telemark options. He daren't trust normal bindings, which were too light.

Bertrand, the French waxman, had prepared the wax for Everest. It was his special *haute montagne* recipe for maximum grip. 'With this on your shoes,' he said, 'you can climb down the side of a skyscraper.'

23

LONG before I ever put on skis, I saw an episode of *The Dick Van Dyke Show* in which Dick Van Dyke goes off on a skiing weekend. He can't ski and Mary Tyler Moore, his wife, doesn't want him to go. You'll probably come back on a stretcher, she says. Inevitably, he ends up in hospital. So desperate is he not to lose face that he has himself patched up and delivered to his door. He plans to bluff it out. Mary has prepared a candle-lit dinner for two and is dressed in a seductive negligee. Dick is fine, he says, just a little stiff. While Mary waits for him in bed, he changes into his pyjamas in the bathroom. He tries to cool her ardour, but she soon sniffs out his guilty secret: he is bandaged up like an Egyptian mummy. He is forced to vow never to go skiing again.

Callahan had seen it too. He didn't think there was any deep meaning to it. 'You never get to see any sex on American TV,' he complained. 'Especially between husband and wife.'

With Callahan it sometimes seemed as if skiing was a substitute for sex; for Cosimo it was the other way round: sex was a substitute for skiing. Medieval saints went up mountains to elude the sins of the flesh and become more holy and get closer to God. Now most of us go on skiing holidays to flirt with temptation. St Moritz promised risks and adventures that were as much moral as physical. In Austria, I picked up a picture postcard of a mountain reconfigured as a woman, with exaggerated promontories and gullies, and men clambering all over her. I sent it to Cosimo, extolling the glories of nature. Ski gear reconfigured you too: the figure-hugging garments were an exercise in covert pornography, designed to envelop the contents but amplify the form, endowing even the most sinewy – men and women alike – with absurdly voluptuous bulges and curves. Mountains were both an invitation to an orgy and an insuperable obstacle in the way of satisfaction. They gave you a woman in a negligee and tied you up in bandages.

In Kitzbühel the best view of the Hahnenkamm, the venue for the fifth World Cup downhill in mid-January, was from the windows of the Krankenhaus hospital, conveniently situated at the bottom of the slopes. The Horn cable-car dropped you off at the door on the assumption that you wouldn't be able to walk very far. There was a church nearby with a graveyard (in fact there were two churches and two graveyards). Lying in bed with your leg in plaster you could see your assailant still lording it over you with his head in the clouds. *Horn*: the German word portrayed the mountain as a bull that has gored a matador or a unicorn that had thrown its rider. The hospital was a gift to the journalist: it was the only place where you could be sure your subject wouldn't slide away from you.

The soothsayers were right: there were more injuries here than anywhere else. Even before I arrived, a lot of contenders had already dropped out. Red Cross helicopters were taking off and landing as if it were a war zone. Crutches were as common as ski poles. Sometimes, the Hahnenkamm was like an assembly line with bodies pouring off the end. At the Krankenhaus everybody was working overtime.

If you stayed here long enough you could count on meeting most members of the US team. Bill Hudson had a room of his own. 'Yeah, we're going to book in advance next time,' he cracked, looking every inch like Dick Van Dyke, but even less mobile. He was one of the score of victims notched up by the Mausfalle. Back in the sixties Robert Redford had played the part of a fictional American skier who comes out of nowhere to win the Olympics. *Downhill Racer* was received with incredulity in Austria, and so too was brash American Bill Johnson when he won the gold medal at Sarajevo in 1984, but Bill Hudson had not relinquished the dream.

The Mausfalle – or Mousetrap – was a form of punishment meted out to anyone who went *off the line*. From the top of the course you could see the skiers take off, pick up speed until they were doing sixty miles an hour going through the second gate after only four seconds, and then dive into a white hole, as if through the platform of a scaffold. Ten seconds later, you saw them again, swerving round a tight right-hander, half a mile below; sometimes you didn't see them again, unless you went along to the Krankenhaus. If they took the wrong line they would fly over the fence and into the trees. Six out of thirteen Austrians failed to finish on the first training run. *Hic peccatores recipit* read the sign above the confessional at the church; but it was to the Krankenhaus that most skiers came to confess and expiate their sins.

Bill Hudson was lucky, he said. 'They were just the small trees, which is nice. I missed the rock.' He had a broken left arm, a cracked right shoulder blade, a compression fracture of the vertebra, a collapsed lung and kidney damage. 'Yeah, nothing major,' he said cheerfully as I read out the list a doctor had handed me. 'Sounds worse than it is: lots of little things. I feel good, just kind of uncomfortable.'

'Will this stop you racing?' I asked.

'Jesus, no. I could do this a hundred times and it wouldn't stop me. I wasn't out of control, I just went right when I should have gone straight. I heal pretty well. I'll be back in six weeks maximum.' Hudson was still pissing blood and seeing double. His face looked as if it had gone ten rounds with Sonny Liston. Callahan examined him with his lens like a doctor with a stethoscope.

A. J. Kitt bounced up and down to test the mattress and eyed a passing nurse appreciatively. 'Looks like you got it cracked here, Bill,' he said. Kitt, a New Yorker who cultivated an unshaven look and jutting sideburns, was the leading American, three years on the tour and starting to get consistent top fifteen results. 'Hey! Our A. J. is really rolling,' Bill Eagan, the coach, whooped when he placed ninth in Val Gardena. 'He's about to bust one out any day now!' His first names, Alva Junior, were enough to explain why he liked to be known by his initials. He thought *Downhill Racer* was a 'cool movie', but said that his inspiration came from his parents, who used to stand him on the tank of their motorbike when he was a kid. 'I just like going fast,' he said. 'I like being on the edge. When I'm not doing something reckless, life seems boring.'

In the main ward, Andrew Christie gave me a Hong Kong lawyer's summing up of the Brian Stemmle saga.

And I didn't have to pay a penny for the consultation. He had alternate legs in the air at the time. He was giving himself traction, pulling on cords on either side of his bed. It had been a shock when he woke up and found he had been stapled like a jiffy bag. Then he remembered the mogul run where the guide had said, 'no drifting'. He and his wife should have been going to Japan, but all the hotels were full so they came here instead.

'Volenti non fit injuria,' he quoted: no harm is done to one who consents. There was a report in an Austrian newspaper that Stemmle was bringing a damages claim against Kitzbühel for ineffective safety precautions. 'I wouldn't want to be handling his case,' Andrew said between huffs as he hoisted a leg. 'He *chose* to put himself there. It's like putting your head into the lion's mouth and then complaining when he bites it off. He knew the risks.'

His left leg thudded into the mattress. 'On the other hand, there is Sunday vs Stratton Corporation.' James C. Sunday filed a $1.25 million suit against Stratton, a Southern Vermont ski area. He claimed that injuries he sustained while skiing there on 10 February 1974 were caused when his ski became entangled in a bush growing at the side of the trail. The defence argued that Sunday was a novice skier whose skis were too long for his level of ability and that he was injured because he couldn't turn when he should have done. The jury took the plaintiff's side and even awarded him another quarter of a million dollars on top of his original claim. On 31 May 1977 Judge Wynn Underwood of the Chittenden County Superior Court issued a ruling that ski operators were potentially liable for all downhill skiing accidents. The immediate effect was to increase lift ticket prices as resorts rushed to insure themselves against similar claims and to enlarge the official exclusion zones on American mountains.

'The trouble with the great American public,' Andrew said, 'is they think somebody has to pay if they get hurt.' He reckoned skiing litigation involving the principle of 'comparative negligence' would be a growth area. It was perfect: you could argue indefinitely over who was more to blame. If you were hit by a car, was he driving too fast or were you not looking? If you were raped, was he violating you or were you leading him on? It was the same with mountains: they encouraged you to get into trouble. Kitzbühel was like a huge department store that had sent security home for the day and invited in a coachload of kleptomaniacs.

I had met Andrew's wife Fanny at breakfast in my hotel. She was a pretty woman with a wide smile and good teeth. He said that she was a better skier than he was.

'She must be – she's not in here, is she?' The voice came from a solid slab of plaster across the room. There was a small round black hole carved into the whiteness where the mouth ought to be. It was like hearing a drain speak.

Andrew asked me to look after Fanny while he was laid up. I promised I would. I took her up the Hahnenkamm in the fog and lost her somewhere on the Steilhang. I never saw either of them again.

The woman at reception said, 'This is our busy period.' Then she added, 'Mind you, summer is busy too.' In winter it was the skiers, in summer the climbers. 'Last year, it was the head, this year it is legs and shoulders.' The broken bodies being trundled past her were like barometers of the conditions outside: 'Last year, ice and stones; this year, more snow.' But there were some things that never changed. 'Always it is the heart.' People came from sea level in the north and went up 2000 feet in the cable car and suffered cardiac arrest before they even hit the slopes.

'Everything is possible,' added Dr Schentner, who had a benign walrus moustache. 'Spine too. Tibia, fibula, knee, hip. In good times, we have seventy to a hundred fresh injuries per day.' Kitzbühel was keeping the medical and legal professions in clover.

As we were going, Dr Schentner called out to us, 'Try not to come back here – *on a stretcher*, I mean.'

'You're not saying much today,' I said to Callahan.

'I'm sure thinking it though,' he said.

Kitzbühel enjoyed a deserved reputation as the most dangerous of contemporary courses. But another Austrian course held the record for the greatest number of injuries in a single race.

In 1936 the World Championships were held one week after the Garmisch Olympics. The weather broke as the Games ended, a thaw removed most of the snow from the Innsbruck course, and a sharp frost on the eve of the race turned what was left to a sheet of ice. Arnold Lunn, a member of the Race Committee, tried to postpone the event until the sun had softened the surface; he wished later he had had it cancelled. Veteran mountaineer Hermann Steuri, who fell twice in the race, declared it more frightening than climbing the North Face of the Matterhorn. The Devil's Glade, a ribbon of polished snow about two feet wide, bordered by a line of tree stumps, accounted for four out of six of the French team alone. The Ladies' Glade ended in a sharp traverse, with more stumps guarding its frontier, leading into the final schuss. The Norwegian Sigmund Ruud, his steel edges skittering over the ice, was hurled into the air by a stump and somersaulted five times, striking the ground each time with his head. Some, including Peter Lunn – who still managed to finish ninth – landed among the crowd. Out of fifty-four competitors seventeen were too seriously injured to finish. Others were hurt, but held on until the finish line, and then fainted. The casualties included three stretcher cases among the spectators, one with a broken leg, the other two suffering from hysteria.

24

SIXTY-ONE – it was the worst start number he had ever had. But for once, Steve Lee didn't mind getting a low draw. 'This is the one place where it's an advantage to ski last. It gets icier and faster. Anton Stahl came from sixty-three to take second.'

Usually, if you started last you finished last. The seeded skiers, the top fifteen, were given priority and the rest of the pack followed. It was an unending subject for debate. Even in the Krankenhaus Bill Hudson and A. J. had been chewing it over.

'It's a mental thing,' Bill said. 'Some guys if they get drawn fifteen, they say – not another bad draw!'

'Yeah,' Kitt said, 'but it's got to be icy as hell to have a chance at the back. If it's soft you're out of it.'

Bill took Steve Lee's side. 'You can still win from the back – in Kitz you can win from fortieth.'

On Saturday morning, from the cabin on top of the 3510 m Streif course, with an 860 m drop to the valley below, it looked as if skiers were diving into a whirlpool. The wind was howling round our ears and the snow billowing up into clouds.

'The course record will go today. It's very fast. So long as the weather holds, I'm in there. My best results are always on the most difficult courses.' I'd never seen Steve Lee so confident before. He had been training with the Norwegian team and referred to himself as 'an honorary Norwegian'. He was a sober realist, no dreamer, but he knew that if he didn't have a shot at the title – which would require miraculous consistency throughout the season – Kitzbühel offered him the chance of redemption. The man who won here was regarded among his peers as the best racer of the year. Hardly anyone remembers who won anywhere else; everyone remembers who won at Kitzbühel. It was the skiing equivalent of Wimbledon: the ultimate test, the standard by which the rest were compared. If you could crack this one, then all those other failures didn't matter any more.

This time Steve was determined. He had even shaved off his lip beard. 'Lower wind resistance,' he said.

'He ought to keep it in a jar,' Callahan said. Callahan lacked faith. He rated Lee's chances as practically zero. 'How can you expect an *Ozzie* to win in Kitz? You might as well ask an Austrian to win in Hawaii.'

Steve was clamping on his boots in a wooden shack twenty metres below the start. The façade was festooned with the ruins of smashed skis going back decades. He was wearing a purple spiderman kit glistening with silver webs.

At the bottom of the course, the hundred-strong Franz Heinzer fan club trooped up and down ringing cow bells. In their red jackets, green pants, and white flat caps, they looked like a phalanx of garden gnomes on the march. Their slogan – emblazoned on their backs in purple – was 'Hupp Franz!' Thousands of Swiss had turned the mountain into a roaring, stamping football stadium.

'My little brother-in-law is a great fan of yours,' I said to Steve. It was too bad George was in the Pyrenees.

'You know I quit the ski team last year. Now I'm an independent. If the Australian team were to turn up right now, I wouldn't even be in it.'

'Don't you ever feel isolated?'

'It's sometimes nice to have ten team-mates – and sometimes not. A team can be a handicap. I don't like to be *under* anyone. The hard thing is not being on your own – it's losing.'

Steve rehearsed the course for me, consulting the map engraved on his brain. The Streif was a downhill with more twists in it than a python and as many bumps as a whole herd of camels.

'Crouched to push off, all you can see between your skis is the horizon, not the track: that falls away under you, almost behind you, like it was concave. You think the first two gates are steep – swerve right and left – and then you hit the cliff. The Mausfalle is a 50-degree drop and 50-metre jump. You've got to keep straight: Bill went off to the right – that was a mistake.' Mentally, Steve was just a few seconds into the race and already he was travelling at 100 km per hour and still accelerating.

'After the jump it's a compression, a double roll and the Panorama turn – a 180-degree left. You can't carve: you have to slam it, do whatever you can to get round. Up over another hill, then dive into the Steilhang. You've got to get the roundhouse right to set up for the Steilhang. It's a hard turn to the left, and the camber runs away from you, then straight down to the fence and the forest. Then start your line across the side of the hill – it comes out on a skinny road, the width of your driveway: the "Woodcutter's Path". It's badly prepared there – the ditch where Stemmle fell. It was dangerous that year. Now they've taken the ditch out and put plastic sheets over the netting. It's still dangerous.'

He thought about his own prospects on the Stemmle stretch. 'If you do it right, you're skimming the net. If you do it wrong, you have to dump a heap of speed. The Bruchenschuss is fifteen seconds on the straight, it lulls you, and then there's a house right in front of you. Come off the road at the Alte Schneise. It's a sidehill, the roughest part of the course. This is where you win or lose. Hold your tuck and keep your speed – if you can. The exit is just bump, bump, bump: difficult to stay aerodynamic. Ease left at the Larcheschuss, then hit the righthander with everything you've got. It's a blind leap at the Hausberg – that's not hard, your first sight of Kitzbühel below – it's what comes after: a hard left with compression. The guys who get it right come through very high. Then jump and tuck – down the Zielschuss – hold your position and you're trying to stop before you hit the barrier.'

That was the theory. In practice, every run was different. It was like riding an unbroken stallion that was bucking every which way to throw you off and you were hanging on by your toes.

This was the course that struck fear into the hearts of the downhill brigade. Literally, Hahnenkamm meant 'Cock's comb'. Fanny called it 'the Wall of Death.' It was first skied by the military as practice for war. Marked out over fifty years ago when it took almost a dozen minutes to get down, it wasn't meant for today's speeds. But it was the Untouchable. 'It's not a race,' Patrick said, 'it's a legend. It's the best – and the worst.'

Some of the men who were gearing up to go were

looking like they had seen a ghost – their own. Luc Alphand, the French skier, said, 'Three minutes before the start your pulse is racing. Two minutes before you wish you weren't there anymore. And one minute before your throat runs dry and you can't speak.' Alphand was right to be afraid: he had to be helped down from the Steilhang by helicopter and was dropped off at the Krankenhaus.

Boris sounded breezy. He knew the course like the back of his hand. 'Yep. I've fallen at the top here, I've fallen at the bottom – and most places in between.'

Even the journalists were worried. The day before, Jules Lapin had successfully negotiated the descent then slipped and twisted his ankle in the public toilets at the bottom. Now he was hobbling around with a stick and talking about suing. It was a bad omen.

'You risk serious injury just watching this race,' said Brian James. He sank thigh-deep into a trough of snow and after digging himself out went off to watch the race on television with a mug of beer in his hand. 'It's safer that way.'

Standing around at the start I felt like one of a host of angels balancing on the head of a pin. I had taken my skis off and lost my footing on the ridge and tumbled down, picking up speed as I went. People flung themselves aside so as not to impede my progress. On my way to oblivion I careered into the steel stanchions supporting a television camera platform. 'Made it!' I exclaimed, and asked the crew a few incisive questions.

Steve said he wasn't scared. 'It's the kind of hill you've got to dominate, or otherwise it'll dominate you.'

There were still twenty-five skiers to go in front of him, but I wanted to be at the bottom when he came in.

'Why don't you wait till he starts?' said Callahan. 'You'll still have plenty of time to make it down.'

'Take it easy, Steve,' I said by way of farewell.

'Definitely not!' he snapped back at me.

I left him intoning his solemn mantra: *let go . . . don't hold back . . . flat out . . . attack.*

I took the cable-car down and skied over to the finish from the Krankenhaus. The Zielschuss was deserted. Had I missed Steve's moment of glory? At the bottom there was sunshine and blue skies, but up at the top the clouds and the mists that at the same time on the same day were blindfolding George in Cauterets had engulfed the Hahnenkamm too, and the race had been put on hold. On the videoscreen there were pictures of the start: it looked as if there was a fault in transmission. An hour later the event was abandoned.

Steve was one of the twenty who didn't get to ski. Flattened to pure ice by the preceding forty-odd skiers, the surface was speeding up and might have given him the record, only everything else was against him. The Italian Runggaldier, who started at thirty-three, came in second. The World Cup wheel of fate had spun once more: while Skaardal was wiped out in the Mausfalle massacre, Girardelli came back to life with an eighth, his best downhill result of the season, and followed it the next day by winning the slalom, watching Tomba lose a ski, and gaining the lead in the overall World Cup stakes.

Boris won the Kitzbühel Cricket Club Cup for the fastest British finisher. He didn't have a lot of competition: none of the others finished.

But it was Franz Heinzer who won the Hahnenkamm, reinforcing and justifying his position at the top of the downhill rankings. Whatever happened afterwards, he was *ex officio* skier of the year. On Saturday night Swiss cowbells rang out in the rowdy streets of Kitzbühel as Heinzer was paraded around town on the shoulders of his compatriots like a Chinese dragon.

'The Ozzie was lucky,' was Callahan's comment. 'At least he can walk away with his illusions intact.'

Steve Lee was feeling so low he contemplated giving it all up. It was his big chance and it had been snatched away from him. He was just a might-have-been. Then he ran into an old friend of his in town, a retired Canadian downhiller named Todd Brooker who talked him out of it. Brooker had come over to Kitzbühel to soak up some of the old atmosphere. There was a picture of him being helicoptered over the rooftops at the end of a rope after he had somersaulted eleven times on the Streif. 'Keep racing as long as you can,' he said, 'because the rest of the world ticks pretty slowly.'

'That's why I'm still here,' Steve said. 'It's like being in the centre of a whirlwind. We're calm, sheltered, sort of immune to things.'

25

In Kitzbühel Callahan and I were staying at the Rainhof, a small hotel adjacent to the level crossing. Frau Gerda, the proprietor, was a broad apple-cheeked woman who was seventy-one and looked like she would live for ever. She still skied. Her idea of a good death, she told us one evening, was having her heart stop as she was 'running straight down in *pulver schnee* (powder snow).' She remembered digging out a dead man from a powder snow avalanche. 'He was standing, his hand up, waving to his partner, who was also killed, and he was smiling.'

Her son, a dark, solemn man, remembered another case of a heavy wet snow slide and the man who was not found for two days. The rescuers spotted crimson crystals on the surface. 'Then they found more blood and they dug following the blood. He was upright and all the blood had drained from his neck. He had twisted it from side to side until it was worn through right down to the bone.'

'Ah, yes,' said Frau Gerda, 'that is so.'

When I set out to ski the Hahnenkamm she said, 'You need always head!'

One morning Callahan and I were having breakfast with Kato, who was a photographer from Asics and wore an Asics one-piece. 'This year, black and yellow flashes on front,' he insisted, sizing up our gear with his bright eyes. 'In Japan, young ladies very good in fashion, very bad in skiing. Crazy!'

Frau Gerda served us coffee. 'Is not good!' she said. 'This time, last year, we have many Americans. This year: one. They all go to Gulf instead.'

'Or the Krankenhaus,' Callahan said.

We were trying to spread frozen butter on dry rolls when three dazzling girls swept into the room like passing comets lighting up the sky. They had just come in from a night on the town, but they didn't look anything like the Heinzer fanclub. Callahan went into shock.

'It's too early for this,' he muttered into his coffee.

We were next-door neighbours but we only ever ran into them on the stairs. When we were going out, they were coming in and vice-versa. We wept bitter tears when they left, feeling like Steve Lee that we had never had our shot. Callahan went pub crawling in town.

Then, as if my prayers had been answered, one of the three came back again complaining she had missed the last train to Munich. I overheard her talking to Frau Gerda. 'I'm going to Munich myself tomorrow,' I said. 'I can give you a lift.'

Frau Gerda said she could stay another night at no extra charge and the girl thanked me warmly and accepted my offer. She didn't have to be in Munich until noon and we would have plenty of time to drive there in the morning. I invited her to dinner and again she said yes and went off to change. *This girl,* I told myself, *will say yes to anything.*

Silvia had red hair and red lips. It was a cold night and still snowing and I deserved a break. On Friday I had arranged to meet an old flame at Munich airport and she didn't turn up. I had eaten alone in a Tyrolian restaurant where I was propositioned by a man in leather shorts.

Kitzbühel after the Hahnenkamm: this was what London must have been like during the Blitz – when you weren't ducking bombers, you were boozing, jiving, screwing. Up and down the narrow flights of steps that linked the broken levels of the old town, under archways, towers and cupolas, there was a terrible sense of urgency among the milling crowds, as if everyone feared they might end up in the Krankenhaus tomorrow. I was no longer a man with a job and a wife and child. I was a born-again bachelor, a sailor docking after six months at sea, a parched explorer who'd sighted palm trees in the desert.

During dinner Silvia nuzzled my ear and kneaded my thigh. By chance, we sat at the next table to the great-grandson of Franz Reisch. Franz Reisch was the first man to bring skis (2.19 m made of ash) to Kitzbühel from Norway in January of 1893. He was the Moses who led the Austrians to the Promised Land. He founded the Kitzbühel Ski Club, became mayor, conceived the first cable-car in Europe, and died with his skis on. Now the name of Reisch was ubiquitous in Kitzbühel: medieval streets were named Reischstrasse, hotels were Reischhaufs and there was even a statue of the great man in the main square. He was wearing a floppy hat and wooden runners eight feet long that rolled up at the end like a snake's tongue. The Reisch family just about owned the place. As Frau Gerda put it, 'they have many hotels and this and this – big, big, big.'

George, the great-grandson, worked for Blizzard Skis – who sponsored Denis O'Brien. He sang the praises of a new compound with a phenolic base that had a high shock absorbency factor *and* elasticity. There was an old compound with the same characteristics: at a conservative estimate, Silvia was upholstered in about three square yards of it.

At midnight I had a rendezvous with Eric, an American ski bum with a degree in history from Yale. He'd been in Kitzbühel for months and was writing a novel about American ski bums in Europe. Silvia and I agreed to meet in the Harlequin disco half an hour later. 'Don't be too long,' she murmured and kissed me goodbye.

By one o'clock I had scoured the shadows of the Harlequin twice in vain. I ransacked a dozen smoky dens and still there was no sign of Silvia. The Londoner, a vast English-style pub with sawdust on the floor, was packed solid with racers and fans celebrating success or survival. Rob Boyd, the tall, anvil-chinned Canadian who had come third, shoved a litre-load of lager at me. 'Have a drink, Andy!' he roared. 'You're off-duty now.'

'I'm looking for a girl,' I said.

'Who isn't?' he said.

The nearest I came to finding her was an Italian named Cristina who was in love with Tomba and boasted of having once touched his bottom. She gave me a sticker inscribed with the words: FORZA ALBERTO – TOMBA CLUB. 'He has such a wonderful body,' she reminisced.

I drove back to the Rainhof and threw stones at Silvia's window. It was my last night in Kitzbühel and I still hadn't broken my duck. The Luftwaffe got me after all.

I would have my revenge though. The bitch could walk to Munich as far as I was concerned. As I was loading my bags into the boot of the Volkswagen, her upstairs window swung open.

'I'm sorry about last night,' she called out. 'I was tired so I went to bed.'

'Same here,' I lied.

'*Auf Wiedersehen.*'

I slid in and reversed the car. As I was pulling out I lowered my window and stuck out a grudging hand.

'*Auf Wiedersehen,*' I heard again. It was another voice, a fake falsetto. I craned my neck round and caught sight of a man leaning out of Silvia's window and waving. He had no shirt on, only a pair of black tights wound round his neck like a scarf. It was Callahan.

26

THE next stop on the tour towards the end of January was Wengen in Switzerland. Some had already stopped and made it no further. Kitzbühel had cut the number of starters for the Lauberhorn; but not all dropouts were victims of the Mousetrap. At the Hahnenkamm, Brian James confided nervously in me. 'Got a call from the office. They want me to go and cover the golf.' He didn't seem very happy about it.

I sympathized. 'Golf? Well, at least it's a change from skiing.'

'Not *golf*,' he spluttered, '*Gulf!* Suddenly they want me to be a war correspondent. Damn it, I'm too old to die! That's a young man's game. I should be in Wengen next week, not Baghdad.'

In the end, Brian developed eye trouble which put him temporarily *hors de combat*. The entire US team was another casualty. After Kitzbühel they received a presidential directive to return home. The White House feared terrorist attacks on unarmed skiers, but as it turned out there was enough terror and death in Wengen even without vengeful Iraqis. The mountains of Switzerland had gulfs of their own.

While other Americans went West, Callahan headed East. 'I've done surfing. I've done skiing. Now I want war. I want to take the Perfect Picture – the one that says it all.' He had visions of global syndication and his name up in lights.

'Do you know anything about the Middle East?' I asked.

'It's mainly sand, isn't it? I know plenty about sand.'

He promised he'd be back in a week, or maybe two. He shot off a couple of rolls on the first training run then took the train to Geneva. 'You want to know the trouble with Wengen? It's too damn British.'

He had a point. Strictly speaking, Davos in the east was the cradle of British skiing; Arthur Conan Doyle crossed from Davos to Arosa on skis on 23 March 1894. But it was the Bernese Oberland that was systematically colonized by pioneering British skiers in the early days of the century.

The father of the Father of Skiing, Henry Lunn (later Sir Henry), who began by selling tennis racquets and became a missionary, first went to Grindelwald (on the east side of the Lauberhorn, a train ride from Wengen) for an ecumenical conference before setting up as the original winter sports tour operator, ferrying thousands of tourists to the Alps every year. His son Arnold spent his childhood summers and winters in Switzerland and put on his first pair of skis aged ten. He boasted that there was no turn on the path from Grindelwald to the Faulhorn he could not recall in the minutest detail, nor a single buttress or rock ridge or snow slope on the great North Wall which was not carved in his memory.

He was an untidy man with an aversion to jazz bands, surrealism, and the metropolis, a classics scholar who left his umbrella on trains. The legacy of a fall in Wales in 1909, his right leg was two inches shorter than his left. It made climbing difficult but encouraged him to take up the cause of skiing with the ardour of a convert and apostle. He was a fervent Catholic who was 'very sure that we shall find on the other side of our last pass the divine originals of the mountains which we loved on earth' and looked forward to skiing in heaven. A Swiss paper christened him 'the Ski Pope'. Three times reported deceased, twice prematurely, he was knighted in 1952 'for services to skiing and Anglo-Swiss relations'.

Lunn was rejected for military service on account of his dodgy leg and saw out the four winters of the First World War in Mürren, looking after British internees and developing his snowcraft and collecting notes for his book *Alpine Ski-ing at all Heights and Seasons.* He was tireless in his efforts to convert others to skiing, but some of the soldiers were sceptical: 'What use is skiing to the British working man?' asked one. After the war, in 1924, it was in Mürren, on the west side of the Lauterbrunnen Valley, that Lunn's Kandahar Club sprang up; on the east side, in Wengen, the Downhill Only Club was its mirror image. Each had its own race: The Kandahar's 'Inferno', as much uphill as down, and the DHO's McMillan Cup, today the last surviving example of the 'geschmozzel' or mass start.

The motto of the Kandahar (named after a town in Afghanistan) was *Sicut sagitta a sagittante*: 'as an arrow from a bow'. The club song spelt out the message:

> But he who will not take it straight
> Down Lone Tree Slope to Menin Gate –
> Why, let the poltroon learn to skate
> And quit the Kandahar.

An old newspaper cartoon has a member instructing his son: 'Always run straight, my boy. It is straight running that has made this England of ours what she is. It will keep you straight in after life.'

The Austrian Hannes Schneider had made a film in the 1920s called *Das Wunder des Scheeschuhs*. He founded a ski school in the Arlberg and his partner, Walter Lent, taught Ernest Hemingway and his first wife Hadley to ski in Schruns. In 1928 Lunn went to see Schneider and cross-examined him closely on the Telemark and the Stem-Christiania turns. Their meeting gave rise to the first of the great classic races, the Arlberg-Kandahar, held alternately in St Anton and Mürren. In 1938 the honour fell to St Anton, but a few days before the downhill Nazi Germany annexed Austria and the Gestapo arrested Schneider, who had expelled a Nazi from the Arlberg School and kept on a Jew. In retaliation Lunn cancelled the race, helped Schneider escape to the United States, and wrote a letter to his Berlin-appointed successor protesting that the Arlberg Club had degenerated into 'a section of the German Imperial Association for Bodily Exercises'.

But the Germans struck back by occupying Norway, the spiritual home of skiing and seat of its ruling powers, and taking FIS hostage. Twice they mounted a self-proclaimed 'International Week' in Garmisch-Partenkirchen, with skiers from the Axis and neutral countries. In 1941 the urbane German hero Caro Crantz took the gold medal before dying a few months later in the snow on the Russian front. Norwegian skiers, past masters in the military patrol event which required you to shoot on skis, joined the Scandinavian Resistance and fought in the mountains. While Lunn became a wandering journalist, eager for action, his son Peter signed up for the British ski battalion in Finland.

Now the Father was dead, but the slim, white-haired, white-bearded son still skied Mürren and offered to take me up the Schilthorn to the Piz Gloria. Peter Lunn was a widely travelled man who only felt at home in the mountains and only felt happy when the earth was wheeling by under his feet. 'A Lunn who does not ski,' he wrote, 'is rather like the Great Auk, now extinct, a bird that does not fly.'

Kandahar Champion from 1933 to 1937, Peter Lunn raced in the Garmisch-Partenkirchen Olympics of 1936 and last captained his country in the Holmenkollen Slalom of 1946. It was his belief, expressed in his book *High Speed Skiing*, that 'when the racer's mind and body are working in complete harmony, he catches a fleeting glimpse of that paradise which was our ancestors' in the Garden of Eden, because he has succeeded in recapturing, if only for a moment, that complete control over the body which was man's before the Fall.'

Peter Lunn still monitored the World Cup in the Swiss newspapers and *The Times* and had heard that Brian Stemmle was suing the Hahnenkamm. He hoped he wouldn't win the case. 'If you fall, it's just between you and the mountain. No one else is to blame. You have to take responsibility.'

He was proud of the Inferno, his father's lasting legacy. It was the longest downhill in the world. The race started at the summit of the Schilthorn (9754 feet) and ended eight and three-quarter miles away at Lauterbrunnen station (2615 feet), and included three short climbs. Every year there were about three thousand applicants. In 1991, 1500 started, two at a time, at intervals of thirty seconds. It took a whole day, from dawn till dusk.

It was a race like no other. Its prehistory, what Lunn

senior called the 'Gothic Spring' of ski racing, lay in chaotic early downhills like the 'Roberts of Kandahar Challenge Cup', where the first man to the bottom might take an hour or more and would act as the finishing post. A. H. d'Egville's account of the first Inferno, in which Arnold Lunn paused on the way down for a cup of coffee and a pipe, neglected to record who had won. Even in the summer of perfected achievement, odd occurrences were not unusual. In 1931, Esmé Mackinnon was approaching the finish line outside the Lauterbrunnen station when she had to stop to let a funeral procession pass by.

Peter Lunn told me another story. After the war, 'Monty' (Field-Marshal Montgomery of Alamein, who had out-generaled Rommel on the sands of North Africa) visited the Lunns in Mürren. It was Arnold Lunn's conviction that 'the Western Powers won the war thanks to their alliance with the S.C.G.B. and the Russians.' The Ski Club of Great Britain included, alongside Montgomery, Hugh Dowding of Fighter Command, Admiral Keyes, and Field Marshals Wavell and Alexander. Montgomery paid tribute to Lunn's role in forwarding the British Ski Year Book to the battlefront: 'I found the snow-pictures very refreshing in the desert.' Towards the end of his stay he rang the editor of *The Times* and said, 'Look, I've never written a letter to the press before. But I want to write one now. It is a matter of great urgency. So I hope you'll print it.'

'Of course,' said the editor, anticipating front-page news of the break-up of Nato, perhaps, or the imminence of a third world war.

This was the letter that I eventually tracked down in the University Library in Cambridge. It appeared on 13

February 1950, and was headed: 'The Decadence of a Noble Sport'.

Sir,

I paid my first visit to Switzerland 47 years ago. I first began to ski in 1925, and in my opinion the general standard of skiing was far higher in those days than it is today. By 'skiing', I mean, of course, real skiing, and not rattling down prepared pistes.

In 1925 a man was regarded as a good skier if he could find his way about the mountains and if he could run fast and steadily on all kinds of snow: soft snow, breakable crust, and unbreakable crust. Today, the one standard of excellence appears to be speed down a prepared course from which every vestige of natural snow has been removed; the result is that for the most part modern skiers are incompetent in soft snow and, therefore, inferior to their predecessors.

Against this decadence, the Ski Club of Great Britain and the Kandahar are fighting a desperate rearguard action. The Ski Club of Great Britain still includes soft snow in its tests and still demands a list of expeditions from candidates for the higher tests. The Kandahar Skiing Club, which originated the modern downhill racing movement, still insists that its candidates shall pass a test in soft snow. It is no credit to the leaders of the various Alpine schools that they should acquiesce in the degeneration of skiing into a kind of glorified tobogganing on wood.

Recently I saw the Inferno Race in Mürren. I also saw it in 1949. This race, like all modern innovations in ski racing, originated with the Kandahar. The Inferno is a test of real skiing. Most other races, including world

> championships, are only a test of piste skiing, a debased and impoverished variant of the real thing. The Inferno Race starts from the summit of the Schilthorn and finishes at Lauterbrunnen 7,000 feet below: the course from start to finish is on natural snow as shaped by sun, wind, and frost. As a soldier, this kind of race appeals to me immensely; it calls for quick decisions; these have to be taken almost instinctively, and this can be done only against a background of knowledge which is acquired only by hard work and a study of snow conditions. We want more races like the Inferno and more badges like those of the Ski Club of Great Britain and Kandahar, which still stand for real skiing as opposed to 'Cresta Skiing'. I appeal to the leaders of the Alpine Schools to do something to arrest the decadence of a noble sport.
>
> Yours faithfully,
> Montgomery of Alamein, F. M.
> Kandahar Ski Club, Mürren, Switzerland

The downhill wasn't the only thing in decline in 1950. In the same edition of *The Times*, gearing up for the forthcoming general election, Winston Churchill declared that the country was going to the dogs under the socialists:

> Times of difficulty lie ahead but I do not fear that we cannot overcome them with good, resolute action and a faithful government not seeking mere popularity, not carried away by some academic, doctrinaire, foreign-bred theme of thought, but trying to deal with the problems that lie around us. I do not doubt that we can find a way of getting back to the high road on which we

were marching five years ago after we had played a notable part in saving the freedom of the whole world.

Montgomery and Churchill concurred in their diagnoses and prescribed the same invigorating therapy: eradicate effete continental influences and revert to sound British tradition. The Inferno was a metaphor for civilization: it was the high road to freedom.

Even Arnold Lunn entitled a chapter of his autobiography 'Regrets of a Frankenstein' and expressed fears that in the downhill and slalom he had created a monster. 'If I have been responsible for the illusion that skiing skill may be measured by pure speed, I owe the world an act of very sincere reparation.' The original conception of downhill, intended to encompass not just varying terrain, orientation and gradient, but different textures of surface – from crust to dust – demanded an advanced education in snowcraft and an understanding of nature in its many moods. Now the snow was packed and hammered into icy cement in the quest for speed and the priority of powder over piste had been overturned and the love of the mountain for its own sake had been all but lost. Lunn felt that the golden age of downhill, the era of the soul skier, ended when it was institutionalized by FIS in 1930. He looked back nostalgically to pre-funicular days when skiing was a means not an end, a passport to the High Alps in winter. Cable-cars, lifts, helicopters were lily-livered compromises that introduced a fatal impurity into the primal experience. They were desecrations of the shrine. '*Où sont les neiges d'antan*?' he lamented.

Worse, the downhill was responsible for the Second World War. Lunn backed the cause of the Church and hence Franco in the Spanish Civil War and only when Germany annexed Austria did he begin to see that the Luftwaffe at Guernica had been rehearsing for the destruction of Europe. The blitzkrieg was nothing other than the downhill applied to military strategy, single-minded all-out attack from the air, a horrific parody of Moses. In some ways, the mountains had set a bad example to humankind. Hitler would have his revenge on the island that had taken over the slopes of Europe and the man who had refused to salute him at the Olympics.

But Lunn enjoyed being bombarded. Straight-running unleashed a spirit of recklessness and the sense of leading a charmed life. He wrote lyrically of dogfights over Dover, of Messerschmitts glinting in the low rays of the setting sun and the hawklike swoop of a Hurricane diving on to the tail of the enemy, and held that illusions vanished in the smoke of battle and left truth behind. Even while the bombs were falling over London, he feared the anticlimax that would follow: 'When the lights blaze from Piccadilly we shall miss the stars which were revealed in the black-out of war. There will be loss as well as gain when the mountains are once more beautiful with the feet of them that bring good tidings and publish peace.'

27

WENGEN is the Land That Time Forgot, an immaculate village that seems to have been preserved in ice, exempt from mutability, for the last half century. Hilton's Valley of the Blue Moon in *Lost Horizon* is partly modelled on the landscape. You can't drive there; motor vehicles are prohibited. You have to take the rack-and-pinion railway from Interlaken that keeps on going right up the mountain.

The Lauberhorn, which provided the four-kilometre course – the longest on the World Cup circuit – for the sixty-first annual international downhill to be held in Wengen, hadn't changed much either. It was known, like the Hahnenkamm, as a 'classic' course (one of the so-called 'Club of Five' embracing Wengen, Kitzbühel, Garmisch-Partenkirchen, Val Gardena, and Val d'Isère) and had acquired its own share of myth and mystique. Conceived so long ago that the first Lauberhorn Cup, in 1930, was won by an Englishman, Bill Bracken, it retained many features that would now be considered technically illegal: the piste was too narrow and rocky and at one point you come swooping through a ten-foot wide tunnel under the railway. At the Hanneggschuss you used to have to jump over a road too, but after a few collisions the scope for disaster was ruled too great and now the road burrowed beneath you. The map of the course had history written into it. The 'Minschkante' immortalized the name of Minsch, who made a record-breaking leap there only to be broken himself. Four Canadians, the entire complement of one year's team, had been hauled in by 'the Canadian nets'.

I was taken down the Lauberhorn by Andrea Cova, who ran the Falken hotel where I was staying and where the summer before Arthur Miller and Peter Ustinov had hosted a conference on the theme of 'How To Solve All the Problems of the World'. 'They didn't solve anything,' Andrea said, 'but they had a good time anyway.' Unable to forget that Arthur Miller had once been married to Marilyn Monroe, Andrea went up to him one day and said, 'You lucky bastard!' He was my age or a little older. His bank account, he told me, was Swiss but his heart was Italian. Whether flying downhill or feeding his great aunt who was ninety-seven and never said a word, his eyes gleamed with a light I never once saw go out. He did everything with passion.

Andrea had raced the Lauberhorn in Jean-Claude Killy's day. When Killy did it in three minutes six seconds he did it in three minutes twelve. This was at the age of only fifteen or sixteen and he had to skip school for a week to train. His performance earned him a place in the Italian youth team. 'Maybe I would have made the Olympics,' he sounded melancholy for a moment and then broke into a grin, 'but I discovered girls instead.'

He recalled the Hanneggschuss as it used to be. 'When I came down there was a guy crossing the road. I had his head right in my sights. Nearly took his ears off. Pity they built the bridge though.' Another year he hit a tree and they took the tree away it was so badly damaged. He thought the course was being made too easy: one section that used to be ten metres wide was now one hundred metres. 'You make an intermediate course, and you make a slalom.'

The descent had been cordoned off for the race and we had the Lauberhorn to ourselves. After a recent fall, it was light powder all the way down, like a cake dusted with icing sugar. Andrea ushered me under the ropes up at the start-hut, with the Eiger like the dark side of the moon behind us and the silver dagger of the Schilthorn, across the Lauterbrunnen Valley, in front. 'Stick with me,' he said. Andrea had won the McMillan Cup four years in a row – eventually they had to change the rules so even if he came first someone else would win – and he was in training for this year's race. He had loaned me a pair of his own skis so I had no excuses. 'Just go straight,' he said. He took hold of my map and scored a thick line from top to bottom cutting through all the curves. 'Slalom – that's for little girls.'

The slalom was Andrea's pet hate. He called Tomba a *mezzo-signorina*. The slalomist was an acrobat – 'you might just as well juggle as you go down' – a ballet dancer. Andrea's body was an atlas of injuries, a chronicle of accidents, and he could identify every contour and feature with the time and place it had been wrecked: 'That rib – it was broken at Cortina in '69. This scar – that is where I was impaled on a pole in '78 on the Mannlichen.' But fractures and torn ligaments were as bracing as a vigorous massage to him. 'I don't feel any pain anywhere now.'

There was something hypnotic about those eyes. They made you do strange things. I didn't time it but I knew I had never gone so fast before. I followed Andrea's line unwaveringly, as if dragged down by a magnet. When we got to the bottom he said, 'Why don't you ski in the McMillan too?'

Wengen clung tenaciously to its traditions, but this year a controversial change was being introduced. It was Denis O'Brien's worst nightmare come true: qualifying rounds. The race on Friday would halve the field and only thirty would go through to the World Cup race itself on Saturday. The knock-out structure would be more dramatic for spectators and television. But a lot of the lower-ranked competitors were complaining that if they didn't make the cut, they wouldn't appear on television and their sponsors would be upset. Steve Lee thought it was a good idea: 'It's tough if you don't qualify. But it's tough anyway.' He was still charged up from Kitzbühel and as hungry to race as if he'd been on a fast. His only reservation was that the thirty who went through – he was sure he would be one of them – should be unseeded, so that everyone would have an equal chance. After Wengen, people blamed the qualifying system for putting too much pressure on the skiers. But the truth was they put it on themselves.

I barely saw what happened. Like everything in downhill, it happened too fast. I almost missed it completely. It was only the qualifying run so I had taken refuge from the cold in Mary's Café at the foot of the Lauberhorn. When I looked up through the thick misted windowpane, all I saw was a spiralling figure on the final bend, a haze of white, and yellow, and red. I finished my coffee before going back out.

There was no hurry, he wasn't going anywhere. Paramedics buzzed round number 44 for a quarter of an hour, then he was stretchered down to the bottom and slid into the Red Cross helicopter. As it lifted off, the blades blew up a blizzard so that people turned their backs and grabbed for their hats.

Gernot Reinstadler was a nineteen-year old Austrian, an up-and-coming all-rounder who had only been on the circuit for a year. His family owned a ski-lift in Innsbruck and his mother was a champion racer. He had a good physique, he trained hard, and he wasn't crazy. I'd run into him once or twice and he was shy and modest and optimistic about his chances. Before Wengen, he had a clean bill of health. He went into intensive care at the hospital in Interlaken where they pumped gallons of blood into him. But his ripped arteries kept pumping it out again and they couldn't keep up. It was 3 am on Saturday morning, the morning of the main event, when the news came through in Wengen that he was dead.

It wasn't until the inquest by television, which obsessively repeated the video recording, that I got a clear picture of his fall. It was *déjà vu,* a re-run of Brian Stemmle at Kitzbühel. Ironically, it happened on the slowest section of the course, on the last S, going through the last gate. After the preceding schuss, you had to lose a lot of speed. Reinstadler hadn't lost enough. It was his first and fatal mistake – everything followed from that.

He was clean through the long right-hander still moving at 70 km per hour and starting to negotiate the tight left when he caught air under one ski and skimmed the gate. He never made the turn that would have taken him down the final straight to the line. He took off right instead and span into the fence legs first. Momentarily he paused, suspended magically in mid-air, then ricocheted off.

Feet first, his legs splayed open in a V, and watched by

several hundred spectators clustered round the finish line below, Reinstadler slid down the slope on his belly, like a raw beginner who has just taken a tumble. Behind him he left a smear of blood ten metres long. Reinstadler was conscious when he slithered to a halt. He lifted his head slightly, as if curious about the state of his body, then passed out.

The protective covering of the barrier that separated the slope from the trees comprised two distinct types of material: the lower half – seamless plastic sheeting – was tough and unyielding, intended to absorb a shock and then bounce back, repelling legs and skis; the upper half – spongy netting – gave gently so as not to break heads and necks. The netting hooked Reinstadler's ski, then threw him back in the snow. The impact rammed his leg up into his hip and tugged it out again, in a clean stabbing motion. Some said the netting was too low. During the night someone went out and raised it another few inches before the insurance men turned up.

It was Gunnar Lindner, the flagman on patrol where Reinstadler fell, who pointed out the exact spot he hit the fence. As the investigators unwound their tape measures, mathematically retracing his fall-line, Lindner said, 'I've seen many dead bodies before. But nothing as bad as that. He looked like a butchered animal.'

He cast his eye over the snow which was still flecked with frozen shards and splinters of red. 'I always hope these accidents are finished. But it is like that in sport.'

It was Patrick who broke the bad news. 'Everything is cancelled,' he said.

'Is it true?' Andrea said, disbelievingly.

'At 5 am the committee met and called off the race.'

'Why the fuck they cancel?'

Opinion in Wengen was split over the decision. Those in favour said it was an appropriate mark of respect for the dead or that it was the only practical thing to do since all the Austrian team would pull out anyway and with the Americans in America and so many injured, who was left?

I didn't need to ask Steve Lee what he thought about it. He had qualified for the race in thirtieth position. He was all dressed up and ready to party and now he had nowhere to go. He was like a greyhound who was never let off the leash.

Andrea was against, passionately against. It was the kind of decision you made at 5 am when the brain is still clouded with emotion. It was bad for skiing and bad for business. Economically, it was a catastrophe. He had 1000 sausages and 500 litres of beer in his tent at the top of the hill. What was he supposed to do with them? Risk was part of the game. There had been fatalities in the past (Patrick reckoned fourteen in major races in the last forty years); there would be others in the future. It could have happened to anyone. A one-minute silence would have been respect enough.

'There are a hundred other resorts begging for this event,' he said. 'Now they will swoop like vultures.'

That evening I found Chris Evert, the American tennis player, sitting on the stairs in the Falken. She had come to Wengen with her husband, Andy Mill, who used to race for the US team and had once fallen in the exact same spot as Reinstadler. 'Andy broke his neck, his back, and his leg,' she said. 'He's still skiing though. He used to laugh about it and do wheelies in his wheelchair. If you want to do downhill you've got to not care what happens to you.'

Five or six men and women were sitting together in the lounge, drinking Andrea's beer and eating his sausages. They spoke mainly in Italian, of *morale* and *morte*, of things that were *terribile*, lapsing into a mixture of French and English. They spoke of others who had died on the downhill, of Michel Bozon, who lining up for the start said to his serviceman: 'Today, *je vais gagner*'; of Count Hubert von Hohenhoe who went through the finish line at Vail in the fog and hit a cable which decapitated him.

'It's a good way to go,' Andrea said. 'Who wants to die crossing the road?'

Sepp Mesner, who was responsible for safety on all the World Cup races, was tormented by the idea that he might have prevented Reinstadler's death if only he had made the sheeting higher. 'I try to think of everything,' he said. 'But this was a big mistake.'

'The only way to make the *discesa* safer is to make it slower – then no one is happy.' Andrea took care to keep Mesner's glass filled. 'He did not have time to feel fear. It's only later you feel afraid. *Avoir peur – c'est la plus mauvaise chose.*'

Patrick was regretting the qualifying system. 'Reinstadler was young and he was pushing hard to qualify – that's why he made mistakes.'

'Twenty years ago,' said Andrea, 'the record for the race stood at over three minutes; now it is two minutes thirty seconds – *voilà le problème*. All of them are killing themselves one way or another. Look at Zurbriggen – his body was wrecked.'

In his front-page article in *La Suisse* the next day Patrick wrote that it was only by overcoming danger that men could become great. He argued that 'you have to stand up if you want to make it to heaven.' He didn't believe it was right to cancel either. But he was prepared to defend the official line. *'Il faut protéger les hommes contre eux-mêmes.'*

Andrea snatched up a newspaper lying on the table in front of him. 'Look,' he said, gesticulating wildly, 'the front page is full of people dying – do they call it off?' He flipped the newspaper over. 'No. And just because there's one more on the back page neither should we.'

'They shit in their pants.' That was Andrea's conclusion. He found one very strong ally in this view. His name was Fred Preston.

'Why all this hysteria when one man dies? It's normal,' Fred Preston said. 'They're all volunteers – they know what they're in for – the race should've gone on. When pilots go out on a raid you don't know if they're coming back.' Fred Preston wore an ecclesiastical collar and described the Lauberhorn as a 'sortie'. He was visiting vicar at St Bernard's English Church in Wengen.

28

FRED Preston was a big man. He was a boxer and a rugby player and he looked it. His face was an old frying pan someone had taken a hammer to. His mother was German. As chaplain to the SAS he had picked up the nickname 'Reverend Rambo' for being more gung-ho than his flock.

The previous summer he had been running a refugee camp on the Iraq-Jordan border. 'One camp I was at, it was total chaos, they were shitting everywhere and dropping like flies with cholera. So the next one I go to, I introduce a bit of discipline and order. Get everyone shitting in the same place. I line them up and tell them: if you don't shit in the latrines, I will personally take you ten miles out into the desert and leave you there. If you make it back, it will be a lesson for you; if you don't, it's a lesson for us.'

The news of his cruel-to-be-kind approach filtered through to England. 'I got a lot of flak for that. You can imagine what they thought of it in Tunbridge Wells. But it worked.'

It was Sunday and we were having an extended breakfast. Fred sounded like a cross between Lunn and Hemingway. 'There is a growing softness among men. Half-men and men with no balls. They forget there are still men who are men. Eventually they'll be stopping children going on the slopes because of the risk of accidents. You see this tendency everywhere – in boxing you mustn't box. All these soft people can say is 'Peace, peace' and throw up their hands like holy virgins.'

Fred had seen a lot of war. He had seen so much blood that he had built an entire morality out of it. There was a picture on television of a plane taking off with a bunch of bombs dangling from each wing. 'Look at that,' he said. 'Isn't that beautiful?'

We kept coming back to the subject of Reinstadler. Fred could never remember his name. 'What they should have said was: "Look, we're sorry about this guy – but he wanted this." You can't train canaries to be tigers.'

I wondered whether downhill didn't automatically entail physiological or cerebral damage, coming down from too high faster than was good for you. 'Codswallop!' he said. 'Look at me – I've regularly jumped out of a plane at 30,000 feet. Has it done me any harm?'

Fred invited me to his service that evening. As he was going he turned back to me. 'You know my philosophy – "Get out there and give 'em heaven!"' And he smote the air with his fist.

Kitzbühel boasted two baroque churches stationed together below the Hahnenkamm. The taller of the two had a slender campanile, the smaller a squashy minaret. Inside, out of the snow, were altars of gold and marble and splendid murals of the Holy Land. In one, like an alpine Sistine Chapel, I found paintings on the ceiling. The central panel showed Christ walking on water and blessing fishermen with one hand. His other hand pointed up into the snow-capped mountains of Galilee where a radiant angel perched in a chariot of clouds.

St Bernard's English Church in Wengen was more

modest. It was a timber turn-of-the-century building, like a barn, painted in white. In the quiet of the early evening I was guided there by the ringing of bells and the contemplative sound of an organ playing. There was an inscription on the canopy wall over the altar: I WILL LIFT UP MINE EYES UNTO THE HILLS. I sat next to Sarah Edmunds, a tranquil English woman in her forties with a dreamy expression on her sensitive face.

The Reverend Fred Preston was wearing a white surplice and over it a black scarf, decorated with military insignia and badges and the wings of the SAS. He addressed the hundred-strong congregation just as he had addressed me at breakfast. He said we would be thinking tonight of our lads in the Gulf and also the Austrian lad who was killed on the slopes. Fred's was the loudest voice in the hymn: 'Guide me, O thou great Jehovah, dear Lord and Father of mankind.'

It was Sarah Edmunds who gave the reading from Romans chapter 8, verses 31–9. She pronounced the words gingerly, as if they were a little too hot for her mouth. 'What shall we then say to these things? If God be for us, who can be against us? He that spared not his own son, but delivered him up for us freely, how shall he not with him also freely give us all things? Who shall separate us from the love of Christ? Shall tribulation, or distress, or persecution, or famine, or nakedness, or peril, or sword? As it is written, for thy sake we are killed all the day long; we are accounted as sheep for the slaughter.'

There was time for one more hymn – Psalm 23, 'The Lord's My Shepherd' – before Fred led the prayers, which almost imperceptibly gave way to a sermon. Instead of asking God for guidance, Fred was asking us for support for the hundreds of thousands of men committed to Desert Storm. They needed our support – it would add strength to their swords – and Fred explained why we should be giving it.

'Once, we were all savages. Then we learned law and order and we became civilized. Without law there can be no order. Just as in sport there must be rules, so society cannot exist without law.

'At first, *rex* was *lex*: when the dictator thinks he is the law. But then there is no law. Anarchy, *an-archos*: it's not when there is no leader, it's when there is no law. Around 2,500 years ago we formed a code: we called it the Ten Commandments. The Roman and Greek civilizations were the greatest after Israel, but still Caesar was king and could commit the most terrible atrocities. Then Christ came and taught us not only that *lex* is *rex*, but that the king must be the primary example of obeying the law.

'He also told us that from those to whom much has been given much shall be asked.

'*Blessed are the peacemakers!* Isn't that beautiful: from the Beatitudes. But notice: it's peacemaker not peace-lover. There's a big difference. Sometimes making peace is not very peaceful.

'*Turn the other cheek!* Yes – but after a while you run out of cheek to turn. Christ himself did not always turn his cheek.

'Human nature is self-destructive. That's why you need the law. I must live under the law or I will destroy those around me and myself. I have to discipline my body: it does not come fit and able for free. I have to discipline myself with my family and my children in case it offends. No one has ever improved on the moral teaching of Christ. But not everyone has learned it and they still have to be taught.

'There are three ways of teaching: through the mind, through the spirit, and through the body. First I appeal to your mind, but you are deaf. Then I appeal to your spirit – and still you refuse to listen. Then you must be restrained through the body. If you bring along your tanks, then I must find a way to defeat you. I cannot allow *rex* to be *lex*, for it will destroy civilization.

'*Thou shalt not kill!* You've got it wrong: what it says is – do not murder. I may have to kill you to restrain you from murdering.'

There was a shuffling of feet and someone coughed. Sarah Edmunds looked at me accusingly, as if I were a zoo keeper who had left the cage door open.

'Freedom is not free; freedom demands sacrifice,' Fred thundered. 'It says in the scripture: without the shedding of blood there is no remission of sins. That is why Christ had to die – for our sins. And until the world is without sin, others will have to die. Many Christians died in the Coliseum for their faith; some will die in the Gulf; some will die right here in Wengen.'

The sermons at St Bernard's were usually only five to ten minutes long. Fred's had been over half an hour. Usually they didn't recommend crucifixion and martyrdom either. As we filed out many of the congregation looked shell-shocked, as if they'd been to hell and back. Sarah Edmunds held on to my arm. 'Fiery Fred!' she said.

'If you can't say it in ten minutes, you can't say it,' muttered another disconcerted soul.

At breakfast the next day Fred provided an explanatory footnote. 'Thank God – or should I say Allah – for Saddam.'

'What?'

'We need bastards like him. To test our mettle. A man like that reminds you what things are really like.'

The Gulf presented an evolutionary experiment, designed to weed out the weak and purify the gene pool. Fred saw everything as an exercise in the survival of the fittest. If you didn't survive, it was because you didn't deserve to and everyone was better off for it. The day we ran out of wars to fight would be a sad day for mankind. Fortunately we were always devising new hazards to face even when we weren't reviving old ones.

'You know, it's funny,' he said reflectively, 'I can box, I can play tennis, rugby, and cricket, I've parachuted from every possible angle. But put me on a pair of skis and I'm like an arthritic octopus. Why is that?'

Chaplains have the highest casualty rate in the army. They are not allowed to carry arms, but they have to put themselves in the front line all the same; you can't administer the last rites to a soldier with a bullet in his head from the safety of HQ. It was the same for Fred in Wengen. The Downhill Only Club took him up the Kleine Scheidegg that morning. The last I heard of him he was completely out of control, like a misguided missile, screaming down towards a mogul field. 'He was fundamentally unsafe,' a witness remarked. 'All guts and no skill.' He was ready to lay down his life. He was more than ready, he was eager.

29

FRED Preston found in skiing a confirmation of all his deepest beliefs; an exemplar of the marvels of Creation, an evocation of the state of grace, a taste of the imminence of immortality, it offered virtually irrefutable proof of the existence of God. For Jean-Paul Sartre, on the other hand, skiing enacted all the tenets of existentialism and proclaimed loudly that God was dead. Sartre was a better skier than Preston. But that didn't prove a thing, since almost anyone was a better skier than Preston.

It was Simone de Beauvoir who introduced Sartre to skiing. According to her autobiographical volume *The Prime of Life*, it was in the winter of 1934–5 that they visited Montroc in the Chamonix valley. The economic crisis was deepening; xenophobia and unemployment were rising; Mussolini and Hitler were poised to slice up Europe and Africa and over the Christmas vacation de Beauvoir and Sartre went skiing. Sartre was working hard on the third draft of *Nausea* at the time and had to have his arm twisted. But the experience was to leave a permanent mark on his philosophy.

They hired some old wooden skis that didn't even have edges. Every day for ten days, morning and afternoon, they climbed up the same slope of the same high meadow and swept down again, tentatively exploring (in de Beauvoir's words) 'this universe without smell, without colour, of a massive whiteness, where the sun sowed iridescent crystals.' A peasant boy showed them how to turn, instructing them in the intricacies of the Telemark and the Christiania. At nightfall, the two returned to their hotel and read up on recent experiments in chronaxia which zapped the nervous system with electricity.

Back in Paris, Sartre had himself injected with mescaline by way of research into hallucinatory images, and soon found himself grappling with an octopus and giant crabs. Unconstrained nature, throbbing and pulsating with life, was guaranteed to induce a sense of horror in Sartre. In *Nausea*, a chestnut tree, heaving with roots and trunk and branches and leaves, is enough to touch off a fit of angst. The philosopher was drawn to Baudelaire's 'Rêve parisien', in which the poet dreams of a landscape cleansed of 'vegetable irregularity', composed of metal, marble, and mirrors, where waterfalls are frozen into crystalline colonnades. Skiing, similarly, represented a kind of salvation, colourless, odourless, inorganic, smooth and shimmering. Perhaps Montroc was the closest Sartre, an *habitué* of the quotidian hell of Le Havre, came to heaven.

Certainly he devoted several pages of *Being and Nothingness*, the 'essay in phenomenological ontology' which he wrote during the War, to an existential psychoanalysis of skiing. Himself a boxer and a swimmer as well as a skier, Sartre took all games, like art and philosophy, to be an exemplification of the human freedom that was his first principle. 'The meaning of skiing' in particular, he argued, 'does not consist simply in enabling me to make rapid movements and acquire a technical skill, nor simply in *playing* by increasing at will my speed and the difficulties of the run, but also in enabling me to *possess* this field of snow.'

The idea of possession leads him to draw an analogy between skiing and sex: snow is like 'the naked body of the woman, that the caress leaves intact and yet troubled in its inmost depths – such is the action of the skier on the real. But at the same time the snow remains impenetrable and out of reach.' Possession is not conquest: it implies not so much overcoming a certain resistance and achieving domination, but rather a fusion with what is possessed. It is less about having than about being.

The main drama of *Being and Nothingness* concerns the attempts of consciousness, the 'for-itself', to leap over the void at its heart and become like the 'in-itself' of matter, which is nothing but itself through and through, inside and out, without ambiguity: in short, to stop becoming and simply *be*. Thus Sartre claims that skiing aspires to the condition of snow. The skier seeks the absolute 'homogeneity' of the substance he slides over. The ideal, the perfect descent, is a 'synthesis of self and non-self', the impossible for-itself-in-itself.

In this sense, all skiing is an attempted escape from reality. The skier wants to give up the responsibility of being human – and therefore always more and less than, say, a waiter, an accountant, a professor – and become for a while a pure *skier*, nothing more or less than a skier, *the* Skier, as elemental as earth and air and fire and water.

But this glorious delusion cannot be sustained. It can only ever last, at its maximum, for as long as you are actually skiing. Transience is built into skiing. 'The solidity of the snow is valid only for me, responds only to my touch,' Sartre says. 'It is a secret that is revealed to me alone and which is already no longer true *behind my back.'*

It is often enough untrue right in front of you as well. Powder, cement, corn; slush, blizzard, avalanche; snow is quintessentially polymorphous, devoid of essence. It is not timeless and intransigent like the earth or rock beneath, but as shifty and unpredictable as a whirling constellation of molecules which never settles down into anything as stable and reassuring as a table or chair. To adopt a phrase of Sartre's: snow is not what it is and is what it is not.

Perhaps then, after all, there is an ironic convergence between the for-itself and the in-itself: the snow constitutes a symbol and a mirror for the skier, briefly holding up the glass to human nature before being rubbed out, exaggerating and intensifying our reality.

Skiing and Nothingness explains, if nothing else, Sartre's fondness for the phrase he quotes at the beginning and the end of his autobiography, *Words*: *'Glissez, mortels, n'appuyez pas'*, which can be roughly translated: 'Glide, O mortals, and don't lay on that edge too hard.'

30

Then, from high up above him, he heard that most dreaded of all sounds in the high Alps, that rending, booming crack! The Last Trump! Avalanche! The ground shook violently under Bond's skis and the swelling rumble came down to him like the noise of express trains roaring through a hundred tunnels. God almighty, now he had really had it! What was the rule? Point the skis straight downhill! Try and race it! Bond pointed his skis down towards the tree-line, got down in his ugly crouch and shot, his skis screaming, into white space.

JAMES Bond was the epitome of the downhill mentality. All downhill racers imagined they had an avalanche on their heels and it was downhill or die. They were all James Bond with a mission to save civilization and marry Tracy Draco.

On Her Majesty's Secret Service was filmed at Mürren (a name derived from the Latin *murus*, 'wall'), the home of the Kandahar. First formed in 1924, it was in February of 1925 that the Club took the train across the valley to challenge their rivals in Wengen. They sported a snazzy 'K' motif on their kit. During the lunch interval the Wengen contingent retaliated by pinning paper badges on their hats and on the badges they inked the initials DHO, standing for Downhill Only.

In the days before cable-cars, it was the railway – the

Wengernalp to Kleine Scheidegg, and the Jungfraubahn, which had hauled itself up the Eiger to the peak of the 4158 metre Jungfrau since the end of the last century – that had first drawn skiers to Wengen. Mürren was for the purists who regularly made the five-hour climb up to the top of the Schilthorn on sealskins or with their skis slung over their shoulders and regarded the long descent as a glorious bonus; Wengen was for irreverent hedonists who couldn't be bothered to slog up on foot. 'Downhill Only Club' was a spur-of-the-moment improvisation which stuck, a provocation, a joke which became an institution.

In 1988 the BBC produced a documentary about skiing (*On the Piste*) which divided skiers into clumsy plebeians and highly skilled upper-class twits. Package tourists in cut-price Austria provided the bottom end of the spectrum, the DHO in Wengen the top. But just as the lumpish proles were played by vacationing repertory actresses, so too the DHO members were framed to fit a preordained script.

The DHO was less a refuge for the idle rich than a microcosm of British society on skis. Company directors were outnumbered by surveyors, accountants, waitresses, a consultant paediatrician from Milton Keynes, and a couple of men, known as 'the Minders', rumoured to be bank robbers. They were not all well-heeled, well-spoken powderhounds. The Club trained youngsters up to represent their countries (Konrad Bartelski was one of its graduates), but it would take anyone who could make it down the hill. It accommodated a wide spectrum of ages as well as skills, reflected in the range of prizes in the McMillan Cup: the 'Bathchair Cup' for the over-fifties, the 'Stretcher Cup' for the over-sixties, and the

'Heavenly Bowl' for the over-seventies. There was a notional award known as the 'Ashes' for the over-eighties, but so far it had found no takers.

The DHO Clubhouse beside the curling rink was a cross between a woodcutter's shed and a cricket pavilion. Alongside a picture of the Queen there were a couple of plaques: one read 'It's an honour to lead', the other politely requested 'Please do not spit on the floor'.

Paul Zvegintzov was secretary of the club. He was a mild-mannered man who appeared as a bloodcurdling Celt in the film *Highlander* and ran an adventure sports school in Aviemore. His other claim to fame was that he had once been centrefold pull-out in *Woman and Home* magazine, modelling an Arran jumper. Everyone called him Paul Zveg.

He showed me the McMillan Cup. On its plinth was graven not just the name of its donor, Flying Officer Douglas McMillan – one of several RAF officers who frequented Wengen in the twenties – but also the date of his death in a flying accident. The British Ski Year Book of 1928 described him as 'a promising young ski-runner who was devoted to the game and would no doubt have gone far.' The first winner of the cup (in a time of twelve minutes thirty-two seconds) and founder of the club, another RAF man, Dick Waghorn, who won the 1929 Schneider Trophy air race in his Supermarine S6, met with the same fate. The late secretary, Piers Benson Browning, a photographer who was a three-time winner of the McMillan, bore on his face the traces of every conceivable variety of accident on skis and in planes and cars. A photograph of him showed a groove down the middle of his forehead the width of a spoon. It took a motorbike crash in Scotland to finish him off. He was a Christian Scientist who objected to helmets on religious grounds.

'You can't stop going fast,' said Andrea Cova, who had lost his driving licence. But now even he had stopped. It was mid-February and I was on my way to Val d'Isère for the next World Cup, but I couldn't resist stopping off in Wengen for the McMillan. Andrea was on his back. He had crashed in training and ricked his neck.

'Andy, I want you to ski the McMillan for me – take my place,' he said.

'I can't do it,' I said.

'You chicken?'

'Callahan isn't here and I have to take the shots.'

'Forget the shots. What's more important – a photograph or the thing you're photographing?'

On the Thursday morning of the race, I took the train up the mountain. The Wengernalp – which beyond Kleine Scheidegg turns into the Jungfraubahn – climbs the steepest gradient of any railway I had ever travelled up to the eternal snows of the highest station in Europe. The train seemed to be built on a hypotenuse, slanted to fit its natural terrain. The seats were slatted wooden benches. There were only two brown and beige carriages, pushed in front of the engine so there was no risk of sliding back downhill. The one I was in was brimming over with Downhill Only people, some hanging from straps or leaning out of the windows, others sitting on one another's laps.

The man who designed the Jungfrau railway, Adolf Guyer-Zeller, died in 1895 of pneumonia and paralysis of the heart before it could be completed, as if the violated mountain, which he had drilled a hole through, was taking its revenge. As the train trundled uphill, I wondered if this was what it must have been like in the tumbril on the way to the guillotine. The DHO skiers joked and laughed about their fate, but they all took the McMillan Cup race very seriously. People slept badly the night before. There would be no television cameras, and there were no money-spinning sponsorships attached, but everyone wanted to beat someone. Who went in for it?

'Anyone who is an idiot.'

The answer came from Mike Loveday, who would come first in the over-fifties category. Looking around the passengers he observed that 'no one is married here. We're all divorced.' There was a high crack-up rate among married DHOs who mostly had room for only one abiding passion.

David Anderson, who was Scottish champion in 1963 and a past winner of the McMillan, boasted of having met Sean Connery at a party. 'I loved that movie where you're skiing against the avalanche,' he told him. 'One of your best.' Connery said, 'I didn't do that one – that was Lazenby,' and walked away. It was a bad film, one of the worst, but for the DHO the mountain sequences made it a masterpiece.

David reminisced about the time he found a ski boot with a foot in it. As we climbed up alongside the grey unforgiving face of the Eiger, so sheer that no snow could cling to it, he recalled that a year or two back there had been a body pitonned to the rock for months. It was said that rescue teams couldn't reach it until the spring, but he thought it was left there to 'act as a lesson to people – like a sign over the door saying, "Abandon hope all ye who enter here."' It was on this monolith that teams of young Germans dangled and died in the thirties for Hitler's prizes.

It struck me that all of us in the compartment had walked through that door, as if that creeping, cranking train was a Titanic on wheels steaming towards the iceberg. Paul Zveg was the starter and the 'sweeper'. I asked what that meant. 'Blood wagon,' Mike said. 'Picks up the bodies.' It was a joke and it wasn't. There was some curious mechanism in us, an internal rack-and-pinion railway, that inexorably hauled us up to dizzying heights and flung us over the precipice.

It was no accident that the DHO had organized the official 'post-race party' the night *before* the race. It was the only way you could be sure that everyone would be able to turn up. But there were drawbacks to the arrangement. Tony Parker was tipped to win and had been celebrating prematurely until four in the morning. He made a bad start, but he was catching up slowly – and then the hangover hit. He was lucky to be wearing a helmet.

The oldest in my compartment was sexuagenarian Henry Lockhart, who was still pissed at the BBC for making them all out to be fools. He'd had a heart operation a month before and was supposed to be lying down. Later that day he was congratulating himself on finishing in front of the lady who won the Heavenly Bowl.

First past the post would be one of the youngest on board, Jamie Anderson, son of David, aged twenty, while eighteen-year-old Sacha Zvegintzov came in behind him. They hadn't been going all out – they weren't wearing their super-aerodynamic gear. 'If Andrea had been in it we'd have had to go a bit faster.'

They were too good to be allowed to win the McMillan Cup though: it was their second season in the Scottish national squad and they were already looking forward to the Olympics. Jamie and Sacha were based in Austria and had trained with Reinstadler. 'These things happen,' Jamie said and looked out of the window. They were in a tight spot: one serious injury and they were finished, but if they were going to hold back they'd never get anywhere in downhill.

While Girardelli was getting two million pounds a year just for wearing the right skis, and the Italian Ski Federation worked on an annual budget of twenty million, the whole Scottish team was trying to make ends meet on a total sponsorship of ten thousand. They were broke. 'You've got no time for girlfriends anyway,' said Sacha.

His father nodded his head. 'You can't afford to get muddled up with girls.'

'What about the Dutch women's team?' Mike Loveday reckoned he had evidence.

Their favourite movies were *Young Guns* – Sacha had seen it twenty times – and *Top Gun*. Anything, in short, with gun in the title. They saw themselves as hungry young gunslingers looking for a showdown with the marshal. But now they had run smack into Jane Russell.

'What makes you think a real woman would look twice at you boys anyway?' Her name was Diana Mathias. She had once skied for Britain and now lived in Colorado. She had the beefy shoulders of a long-distance swimmer and rippling legs. Even Fred Preston, who used phrases like 'the weaker sex', described her as 'a woman with balls'. Diana had a penetrating gaze that was always sizing you up. It was like looking into the lens of a theodolite. She had a habit of asking probing questions. 'You're not actually skiing, then?' she said to me.

The train disgorged its passengers at the Kleine Scheidegg station and we took the Salzegg chairlift over to the start. If the starting line had extended sideways another half a mile, it would have run into the jagged, prehistoric geometry of the North Face, which seemed to lie in perpetual shadow. To the west, the Jungfrau ('Maiden', so named by the monks of Interlaken because it reminded them of white-robed Augustinian nuns), though some six hundred feet taller, still called on the snow-cowled Monch ('Monk') as chaperone. The impeccable pyramid of the Silberhorn, sitting on the left hand of the Jungfrau like a metronome, counterpointed the rugged reality of their imperfections. These mountains seemed like a catholic anthology, embracing Gothic and baroque and romantic, dolomitic towers, Gaudi spires and frozen hurricanes. On the east side of the range the Rhône glacier flowed south towards Marseilles. A couple of miles straight down was the town of Grindelwald where, a century previously, Henry Lunn sought to reunite Christendom.

Callahan had given me a roll of Fujichrome 100 and specified the settings: I jiggled the shutter speed round to 500 at f11.5. Through the lens I saw Paul Zveg unfurl an enormous Union Jack and flap it over his head. Beyond him in a tidy line, framed by the Eiger, were fifty men, women, and children. He dropped the flag and I pressed the button. When I took the camera away from my face, the straight line had melted into a stream that flowed away downhill. A dozen or so at the front had a mental avalanche on their heels and pointed their skis at Grindelwald. Behind them the pack were already plotting crowded diagonals. At the start, a handful were still writhing in the snow: they had turned too soon. The geschmozzel start punished timidity. The McMillan was not one race but several races run concurrently. It offered almost infinite variations on winning and losing.

I slung the camera bag over my shoulder and took off down the hill. The snow was soft and yielding and the first five hundred yards was a narrowing gully between converging lines of trees. I took it straight. Slalom was for little girls. The secret to any race is to know the course like the back of your hand. I had no idea where I was going, other than down. The light was flat and grey and the camels were upon me before I knew it. For a moment I could see Denis O'Brien on the OK at Val d'Isère and I saw myself sprawling in a shamrock helmet, then I sailed free over the ledge of the incline.

'Keep to the left,' I remembered Mike Loveday saying. 'That's the key.' I clung to the left as I shot past an SOS station where several skiers had pulled in for repairs. An S-bend opened up in front of me. The left-hand side was all ice and bumps so I let myself float out to the right. A primeval rock face sprang out at me, glowering at this deviation from the line. Suddenly I was in the gutter with Brian Stemmle and frantically digging in my edges to carve my way out again.

This course was a compendium of the courses I had seen. It even had its own Mausfalle. It would have been wiser to ease up and take a look. But a force stronger than reason rushed me unheeding towards the void, the wind shrieking in my ears. Bill Hudson had angled right on the Hahnenkamm and smashed into the trees, so I angled left. Flying over the brink I wished I'd angled right. It was like going over Angel Falls. Below me, miles below, was a steaming torrent, backed up by a bristling forest.

Lunn said: you never fall, you only *choose to fall*. I had already chosen to fall when my skis plunged into deep deep snow and I weighted hard, swerved right and juddered back on to the path. The hill flared out into undulating fields, a railway track in the distance, the roofs of Grindelwald. I pointed my skis straight down again and held my tuck for the final schuss, my poles twin exhausts behind me. Exploding over the line, my skis spouting snow like smoke from burning tyres, I span round to glare at the clock. As I punched a hole in the air I could hear a distant ringing of cowbells.

31

On the summit of the Mountain of Purgatory Dante was reunited with Beatrice; in the lamasery of Shangri-La Conway found Lo-Tsen; on the parapet of the Reichenbach Falls Sherlock Holmes joined with Professor Moriarty. In Wengen I met Izzie Slater. She stood at the front when I took a picture of the survivors. She was small and slim like a ballerina and when she shook her long dark hair out of her hat it came down to her waist. After losing a ski and putting it back on again, she finished around fortieth and won the women's 'Open' category. She was in a category of one: the only resident female racer. She worked in a hotel in Wengen. Once she had worked for Andrea Cova, but walked out claiming she'd been ripped off, robbed, swindled and cheated.

After lunch we all skied down to the railway station. But when the others crammed into the train going back up the Scheidegg, Izzie pulled me on to another train. She wanted me to see the Blue Glacier Pass, she said, where Lunn used to ski. We descended on to an empty platform, clicked into our skis, and zigzagged up through thinning trees. A brook had broken through its lid of winter ice and the snow was sprouting clumps of *perce-neiges*. We came out on a transparent ledge illuminated by a blue light within, overlooking a frozen lake thousands of feet below. 'The slopes between here and the valley face south,' she said. 'You'd think it would be all sun-baked crust. But, look, you can see they're intersected by ridges. On the short north slopes we'll find powder.'

Sure enough, the crisp swish of the steep spring corn – melted and frozen again – yielded intermittently to a velvet rustle. When the finely sieved snow billowed up in our faces, it felt like being wrapped in a cloud. We chalked up a column of linked figure eights and hooted like five year olds as we swung round to admire our criss-crossing curves. When my skis broke through a hollow crust and I was thrown down she stood over me and, laughing, prodded me with a ski-pole. As the light faded and the snow turned orange, then purple, as if we were skiing down a rainbow, we shivered in and out of the fringe of pines which tonsured the town, lit up below us like a constellation of stars.

Later I saw Izzie again in a restaurant in Wengen. She was wearing tight black denims and having a conversation over dinner with a short man named Geoffrey.

GEOFFREY: You have no ambition.

IZZIE: You have too much.

GEOFFREY: Why are you an atheist?

IZZIE: There seems no good reason not to be.

GEOFFREY: Come back to London with me.

IZZIE: I like it here.

That night the bar of the Falken played host to the Vulgarian AGM. The Vulgarians were a sub-sect of the DHO and their president was Andrea Cova. The main qualification was a willingness to wear a coal scuttle over your head while singing. At one time there were a dozen singing coal scuttles seated on the bar-room stools. Izzie wanted to get out. She had an unnatural fear of men in coal scuttles, especially Andrea Cova.

We crunched along the narrow path that led away from the hotel. Out of the moonless, star-hung sky a pale blue sheen fell upon the dome of the Jungfrau and the new-laid snow was phosphorescent beneath our feet.

'I'm too much of a coward,' she said. 'I only once went completely flat out.' She pointed to the waning scar on her cheek that she had picked up two years before in the Heinz Cup at Innerwengen when someone cut across her path.

'Cowards don't have scars,' I said, pulling her under a lamppost and frowning to exaggerate the pallid Hawaiian crescent over my left eye. 'Once is enough.'

Izzie had graduated from Oxford in Chinese and wrote a thesis on Deng-Xiao Ping, the Mr Big behind the massacre in Tiananmen Square. Izzie thought he wasn't as bad as was made out and quoted a favourite dictum of his: 'It doesn't matter if the cat is black or white so long as it catches mice.' She was introduced to the DHO by her ex-boyfriend who could speak backwards fluently. Not just reversing the order of sentences, but the letters of every single word within it, like a book read from back to front. They had met on an artificial ski slope in Harrogate. 'He was a genius. Went completely off his rocker in the end.'

At the Carousel bar, Izzie requested Marvin Gaye's 'Sexual Healing' and told me she hadn't been too impressed by the Great Wall of China.

When we got to her apartment she invited me in. I was faintly surprised not to find Callahan there. But if I couldn't see him I could definitely hear him.

Izzie showed me her 'list of misdemeanours' drawn up for a court case against former employer Andrea Cova. He came out of it worse than Deng-Xiao Ping. The list was twelve pages long. It was a thesis.

There was a deep pile of A4 paper on one side of her desk. It was covered with writing.

'Another Cova?' I said.

Actually, it was notes for a novel based on Izzie's experiences, to be called *What Will The Weather Be Like Tomorrow*?

'What do you think of the title?' she said.

'I think it's great,' I said.

'You won't steal it, will you? Promise you won't.'

'I promise.'

'You only want me for my titles.'

My twin brother Unc once explained to me how, scientifically speaking, it was possible to ski. 'It's all to do with melting point,' he said. 'Snow is frozen water. When you apply pressure, the melting point goes down, so it turns back into water. Essentially, when you're skiing, you're really walking on water.'

The human body is mainly frozen water. It has a melting point too. Under pressure it reverts from the solid to the liquid state.

32

ANDREA got up to see me off. He was still pretty creaky, but he was already looking forward to next year's McMillan Cup. 'Tell them I'll be back!' he said.

I took the train with Elja. She'd had a dream in which she was turned into a wolf and screamed for help, but she had been slowed down like a 45 rpm disc played at 33 rpm and all that came out was a low-pitched growl that no one could understand. She was reading a book entitled *Masochism: Current Psychoanalytic Perspectives*. She had highlighted so many passages with her yellow marker pen that the unmarked bits looked like little white oases in the desert.

As the Wengernalp abseiled down the hill to Interlaken, the falling snow drifted against the windows and blanked out Switzerland.

When I arrived back in Val d'Isère the snow was still falling. Forty days and nights before, Val d'Isère had been duffled up in a white overcoat; but it was possible to have too much of a good thing: now it was smothered in a straitjacket. The same time last year the Club des Sports was moving mountains to stage this event, trucking in snow from a hundred miles away to clothe the bare slopes; now it was trucking snow out again in a desperate effort to strip them down to a hard, skiable surface for the race.

The roads were blocked coming out of Geneva and I turned up late, worrying about how much I had missed. I hadn't missed a thing. It was a white-out. This time the World Cup was using the new Bellevarde piste, the Face, brainchild of Jean-Claude Killy and Bernhard Russi and venue for the 1992 Olympics.

Russi, from Andermatt in Switzerland, was a double gold medallist at both the 1970 World Championships and the Olympics two years later. Between 1970 and 1977 he won nine World Cup downhills. In 1978, at the age of thirty, he retired from skiing to return to his first career as an architect. But within a year he was back with a new job, whose previous incumbent had been God. This time Russi was designing not chalets and hotels but mountains; FIS employed him to lay out new downhill courses and revise the old ones. Elja introduced us in the giant marquee at the foot of the Bellevarde that served as a press centre in Val d'Isère. He was fit and bronzed and rugged with a furrowed brow. He was as nervous as a father whose child is about to go on stage for the first time – or on trial.

In the golden age racers were free to carve out their own manic path back to earth. Now the downhill course marked out an obligatory and collective itinerary, but it implied only minimal interference with the natural fall-line. The undeviating linearity that the downhiller aspired to was always just an imaginary limit, a utopia of maximum gravity and speed; on any mountain you would have to negotiate shifts in terrain, variations in snow, bumps and humps, crags and crevasses, narrow passes and the abyss that beckoned beyond the brink. The classic courses of Kitzbühel and Wengen incorporated all the complications of reality.

Russi thought the one big mistake since the war had been to diminish the reality principle. As techniques and equipment improved, skiers went faster and downhill became more dangerous. 'What did we do? We went to the great pistes and took away the tough bits. The result was that skiers went even faster, so now it is more dangerous than ever.'

'What about Wengen?' I said. 'Reinstadler died on the slowest section.'

'It is still too fast. The trouble is not the S but everything else before the S. My fight is to cut down the *average* speed of races.'

Unhindered acceleration down a smooth highway induced a sense of unreality, of living a dream of domination and omnipotence, so that when the skier came up against a sudden minor asperity, a fold in the fabric, he collapsed like a punctured balloon.

'Who are you fighting?'

'The skiers. And their coaches. In the evening, around the bar, they agree the sport has become too fast. But in the morning, when the competition is strong, just try and change the course to hold them back – they won't let you.'

In this sense, downhillers were like tennis players. Intellectually, the top professionals agreed that enhanced racquet technology produced too many aces and was in danger of reducing the game to sheer power play, a battle between annihilating serves. They talked about depressurizing the balls, banning wide-bodied racquets or redrawing the service line; but join two men in a match and each would try to blast the other off court with a handful of bullets.

Russi never won at Kitzbühel or Garmisch. He performed best on the straighter, smoother courses. But now he wanted to make life difficult for the straight runners. Downhill was always a dialectic: you wanted to get down and the mountain thrust massively back up at you and got in the way; sometimes you slotted into the perfect trajectory that seemed to cut the resistance to zero. Heinzer had the ability to find that line where man and mountain merged and ceased to struggle against one another. At Val d'Isère Russi was bent on increasing the resistance factor.

'The Face de Bellevarde will frighten many. But only the best can win here. I make the great prove their greatness, show *all* their skills. This is not a piste to fly down, be lucky, and win a medal.'

In the summer Russi and Killy had slowly explored the 2,905 metres of the Face on foot, edging down the vertical drop of 972 metres with extreme declivities of steeper than 1:2. They christened the parts of its anatomy according to geography, history, or the vagaries of chance: Partridge Rock (a bird with a broken wing had its nest here), Eagle's Bend (whose guardian could sometimes be sighted hovering overhead), Catherine's Hump (memorializing a Val d'Isère woman who had died young), Edelweiss Wall.

Some of the finer points of architectural reasoning and nomenclature were wasted on the skiers. A lot of them didn't like the Face. They were objecting that the downhill was a super-G in all but name, less a straight line than a cramped intestinal zigzag, virtually a Tomba-tailored slalom, for which the manufacturers had had to produce an *ad hoc* 'Bellevarde' ski, specifically tailored to accommodate its oddities. There was even a sinister rumour to the effect that it was all intended to improve the chances of the French. Franz Heinzer, fresh from another victory at the FIS 'World Championships' in Saalbach (a separate one-off event), wasn't complaining. 'It is a good course for me,' he said after a training run. 'Some don't like it because it has twenty-five corners; but Kitzbühel has fifty.' There was nothing nature or Bernhard Russi could throw at him he couldn't withstand and overcome.

Even if opinion among the competitors was mixed, at least the multinational fans crowding into town for the season's last downhill in Europe should have been happy. Russi's revolution consisted, in part, in giving a clear view of eighty per cent of the race from the foot of the mountain – far more than anywhere else – and thus making it possible to grasp the totality of the event. And by subtly obstructing the descent, nuances of technique and differences in style would become manifest. The Face would be a revelation.

There was only one catch: the spectators could see, but the skiers couldn't. Unless there was 100 per cent visibility, they were skiing blind.

Russi had devised a technically brilliant, fiendishly difficult geometry, with corrugations and twists and chutes – but had forgotten to build in any landscape. The Passage d'Ancolie, cut specifically to preserve a rare species of Alpine wildflower, deep blue with five petals, was held up as an emblem of an ecologically sound approach that blended the course with the natural contours and properties of the mountain. Unfortunately, while the flowers were given five-star accommodation, the trees had been bulldozed to make for an uncluttered line of sight from below.

When you removed the mask, the Face was faceless,

there was nothing to reveal but nothingness. Now, looking down from above, and moving at speeds that made everything a blur anyway, there was no relief, no contrast, no features to pick out the right line of descent. If it was snowing, it was like skiing inside a feather pillow with cotton wool over your eyes. Fearless, devil-may-care downhillers degenerated tragically into tottering old men with failing eyesight, poking their poles out before them like canes probing the darkness. For the Olympics perhaps the Club des Sports would truck in some trees.

To compensate for the loss of Wengen, two races had been scheduled at Val d'Isère. After the first, on Friday, was cancelled, there was optimistic talk of conditions easing over the weekend, but in reality the falling snow, initially just a fine sprinkle of talcum powder, by Saturday was thickening like porridge. Patrick Lang and Steve Lee, Callahan and Cosimo, the Canadians and the Japanese: they were all ghosts vanishing into a dancing, swirling, hexagonal oblivion. As if in a dream, a colossal inflatable Evian bottle swam towards me, attended by a giant G&M jelly bean.

So it was that I could hardly take it seriously when Marc Girardelli materialized by my side. I had been looking for him for months and now, miraculously, he had come to me. I took him at first for just another balloon, with pumped-up muscles, a silver moustache and blue eyes like headlamps.

'All you can see up there is white, white, white,' Girardelli complained. 'It is impossible today – and impossible tomorrow too. All you could ski in this is slalom. Downhill would be murder.'

Girardelli recalled how he had started his career in

slalom: 'I wasn't naturally a downhiller,' he said. 'I chose to do it – to extend myself.' Then he vanished once more into the mist.

The weather was closing in all over the Alps and a white darkness was descending. Soon no one would be able to get in or out. Not waiting for news of the inevitable cancellation, I caught the last bus out of town, like Humphrey Bogart quitting Paris before the Nazis crunch in, leaving Ingrid Bergman behind him.

I'd done the European leg of the World Cup – or what was left after the mountains had taken their toll – and I was broke. Simon O'Hagan hadn't wanted an obituary from Wengen. 'There are enough dead bodies on the front page,' he said. For want of anything better, he'd taken a paragraph on the weather at Val d'Isère. And he was doubtful about any more reports. There was no word from Callahan and it looked as if the ski bum's grand tour was over for both of us. I was even a little tired of skiing. But in Cambridge I was soon dreaming of myself back on skis, the way an amputee imagines his limbs are still attached.

'You don't need a peak to have a peak experience,' Heather reassured me. 'I can have a peak experience just falling asleep at night.' She lived on a higher plane and was doing her best to haul me up alongside her.

Our son was trying to stand up. He had strong legs, but it was far too soon and he was always falling down again. He had mysterious reserves of energy and cried out against the coming of the night.

God called on Abraham to take his only begotten son Isaac and make of him a burnt offering in the mountains of Moriah. In complying with Callahan's imperious command to go into the Alps, I had been symbolically sacrificing my son – or offering to sacrifice myself. A pair of skis was an altar with bindings. Like Oedipus's father, I had exposed my son on the mountainside, but there was no escaping my own fate.

This time it was Cosimo who left me no choice. 'Your analysis is based on an incomplete sample,' he said. There were two more downhills to go in March, the last but one in the States, and the last of all in Canada. If I wanted to catch up with Uncle Pat and prospect for gold, it was now or never. So I scraped up an assignment in Los Angeles and scrounged a flight from Virgin.

33

IN Los Angeles the black immigration officer could have been a retired basketball player: he was sitting down and still he towered over me. 'What is the purpose of your visit, sir?' he drawled. 'Is it business or pleasure?'

'Business.'

'What kind of business?'

'I'm covering a skiing contest in Aspen.'

His eyes lit up. 'Were you covering the Gulf?'

'No.' I felt obscurely that this constituted a dereliction of journalistic duty, so I added, 'I was tied up.'

'Would you have liked to be there?'

Clearly, this was a test of some kind, instituted since the war. 'No,' I said. I didn't know if I had passed or failed.

'Ooo-wee,' crowed the immigration man. 'That would have been some dangerous mission, huh, sir?'

When I went to pick up my ticket for Aspen the next morning I couldn't help noticing the posters advertising blue seas, grass skirts, and cheap flights. I was jet-lagged and susceptible. I asked if I could trade in my Aspen ticket for a round trip to Hawaii. No problem. All I had to do was keep on flying west instead of cutting back east inland. It wasn't too late to catch some winter swells on the North Shore; the whales would be surfing in Waimea Bay; I could do with taking my clothes off for a change. I felt cold in my bones from spending too long in the wilderness. And anyway, there were mountains in Hawaii weren't there? I remembered seeing an observatory up above the clouds near Kaena Point. My twin brother Unc had been offered a job there once and turned it down. Was I going to reject another golden opportunity?

As I boarded the plane for Aspen, I felt bad about not giving way to that impulse and I would feel a lot worse later. There were no rooms left anywhere in Colorado and I wound up in the dormitory of a hostel on the edge of town called the St Moritz.

In the 1850s John A. 'Snowshoe' Thomson (born Jon Thorenson at Telemark, Norway in 1827) used to deliver the mail to miners digging for gold and silver in the hills and could ski ninety miles in two days carrying loads of sixty to a hundred pounds. He would sleep the night in caves or abandoned cabins and scorned blankets. Butch Cassidy, on the run from the law, holed up in these parts. Later, Arnold Lunn, eluding Hitler and the Blitz, attended the annual dinner of the Colorado Arlberg Club in Denver. He was reunited with Hannes Schneider and they officiated at the Far West Kandahar Challenge Cup. A band struck up the Mürren Waltz but Lunn found 'it was as difficult to believe that Mürren still existed as to realize that powder snow lay deep in the Blumenthal when Christ was born.' He was on a coast-to-coast lecture tour counselling the United States against isolationism and exhorting Americans to take a more active role in the fight against Nazism and regard the war in Europe as their own. Now Kuwait had become the front line of freedom and smart missiles from California sniffed out targets in Baghdad.

On the night I arrived in Aspen there was a press party at Little Nell's Saloon. There was a banner swung across the rafters: 'LITTLE NELL'S WORLD CUP BASH'. Patrick was sitting on the floor, his cowboy hat flipped over the back of his head, his immense legs drawn up into leather-trousered triangles.

'Mr Martin! Are you crazy?' It wasn't really a question. 'You arrive late again – you miss it all.'

'What have I missed?'

'Only the most exciting downhill of the year and a great GS.'

'I got held up – I meant to get here earlier today.'

'The downhill was yesterday, today was GS.'

I slumped down beside Patrick. I had just travelled halfway round the world for nothing. 'And tomorrow?'

'Tomorrow we take down the tent and depart. Tomorrow is Canada. You coming?'

'I'll stick around for a few days and catch up with you later.'

'You're going to love it here. The greatest powder in the world, like silver dust, like cocaine.'

He stuffed a bottle of beer in my hand and I wandered out on to the verandah to clear my head. Heinzer had won the Aspen 'Winternational', beating Skaardal into second place again. After losing first Wengen and then Val d'Isère the World Cup committee had arranged a second downhill at Lake Louise, making it still mathematically possible for the Norwegian challenger to overhaul the leader. Skiing on only one good leg Girardelli finished thirty-seventh and still had to face Tomba in the slalom to settle the overall title. I came in last.

The hotel was right at the foot of the mountain and the slopes above were illuminated with floodlights. A 'synchronized skiing' demonstration was in progress: a team of skiers known as the 'Aspen As', 1990 world champions at Vail, in red leotards with smoke machines strapped to their backs, were arcing across the snow like trapeze artists and pulling off spectacular somersaults and 360s. It was like watching Alberto Tomba in quintuplicate. Over an invisible public address system, like a voice from the clouds, Larry was providing the commentary.

'The Aspen As. Aren't they terrific? Guys, we appreciate you more than you will ever know. This is great skiing. What a pleasure it is to be here. You're such great company. Thank you, Dick, for a truly great show. And a special thanks to the Aspen Fire Department – you people are just the best.'

The throb of 'Johnny Be Good' gave way to the opening bars of 'Also Sprach Zarathustra'. 'Thank you, Dick, for some great music. Ladies and gentlemen, we love having you here. Boy, have we got a party going. This is so good, I'm stoked! I'm feeling good!' The word *good* had about ten 'o's in it.

The Aspen As had finished synchronizing, but Larry didn't take any notice. The less that happened the more excited he became. 'You're wonderful all of you! Thank you Dick, thank you Victor, thank you Bob.'

I ran into one of the Aspen As. His name was Riggs Klika. He spelt it out for me. 'Andy Martin!' Riggs said in astonishment when I told him mine. 'You're Andy Martin? We got an Andy Martin in our team. You're not related are you?'

Fireworks were bursting all over the night sky in Aspen. I was coughing and my voice was going as I shuffled back to my dorm at the St Moritz. In the morning I was barely alive, white with sickness and starting to hallucinate.

Sam, the amiable Texan in the bed next to me, leapt up and flung open the curtains. 'Hey, great day out there, fella,' he boomed in my ear. 'How are you feeling? You're sure looking a lot better anyway.'

It was hours later when I rolled up all my strength and slumped into the bathroom. I think I was lying in a heap in the corridor when a well-filled salopette went by. 'Could you do me a favour?' I gasped.

'Huh?'

'I wonder if you could ask the front desk to send someone up with a glass of water?'

'Plenty of water right there in the bathroom, buddy.' He was already in his ski boots and impatient to be off.

'Right – but do you think you could ask them anyway?'

'Ask them yourself – dial O on the phone.' And he was gone.

Pascal said that all man's troubles stem from a single cause: his inability to remain at rest in his own room. He argued that war and sport and sex were elaborate *divertissements,* intended to take our minds off the contemplation of our own futility and nothingness. The thing was to shut yourself away from all those pointless distractions and settle down to reflect on the terrible truth about the universe. For three days I was manacled to my bed, but war and sport and sex regularly came in to see me and visiting hours were unlimited.

Dave Leonardi, the editor of *Skier News,* consoled me. 'At least it's an English-speaking country,' he said. 'I'd sure hate to be sick in Japanese.' He brought me back a 'sure-fire remedy': a can of Coke and a tub of ice-cream.

'Works every time. You have to avoid the fancy flavours though. Stick to vanilla: it's easy to digest, it'll give you energy, and it'll coat your stomach.'

Kieron was a marine biologist from Scunthorpe who couldn't swim. He told me Scunthorpe meant 'town of Scun'. Scun was a Viking who came over to England to rape and pillage, liked it and stayed on. 'He started a tradition,' said Kieron. 'Scunthorpe is a rough old place.'

When Sam heard I was a writer, he said, 'Hey, why don't you write about Being Sick in Aspen? Yeah, you could make a series out of it – Being Sick in LA, London, Paris. There's an untapped market right there. You can talk about all the guys you met in your dorm.'

'Do you think that'll be interesting enough?' I croaked.

'Sure it'll be interesting!' he exploded.

Conversations on the other side of the walls would break in, like stray signals from foreign radio stations, and then annoyingly fade out at the crucial moment:

'I don't usually like to reveal this about myself to other people, but the truth is . . .'

'None of my girlfriends ever asks me to do that . . .'

'Motherfucker!'

'The Lord be praised! Thank you for this situation.'

'Tomba! Tomba!'

I never got beyond the headlines on the sheaf of publicity brochures by the side of the bed:

ASPEN IS AN ENDLESS PLAYGROUND FOR WINTER VACATIONERS.

ASPEN HAS THE FINEST SHOPPING AND DINING IN THE WORLD.

ASPEN – DON'T MISS OUR SUMMERS! YOU MAY NEVER WANT TO GO HOME AGAIN.

On his eighty-day journey round the world, Phileas Fogg left all the sightseeing to his valet Passepartout. I was served with equal zeal. Dim, anonymous figures would burst through the door jabbering, 'It's waist-high powder out there and only five guys on the slopes!' Through my window, which had thigh-wide icicles for bars, I could see Cathedral Peak in the distance and, closer, Aspen Mountain, rounded, immaculate, unlined, waiting for me like a bride. But I wasn't going to make it to the wedding, I was sliding down, down, down into a white transcendence.

When I woke up I was better again. I felt as well as I ever had in my life. I had been dreaming of Callahan and Cosimo meeting up and now it was coming true. Cosimo and I were on our own but I knew Callahan would turn up soon. We were climbing side by side up a steep face on sealskins. It was like skiing uphill, smooth and frictionless, almost as if gravity was operating in reverse. The sun was smiling down out of a clear blue sky and fresh snow whispered beneath our skis. As we approached the peak, there was a clattering noise above us and we looked up into the heavens to see a helicopter whirling overhead. Callahan was being winched down to earth on a rope ladder. We coincided, all three of us, on the summit.

Cosimo gazed at Callahan and Callahan gazed at Cosimo. I had often speculated about what they would say to one another if they ever met. Would there be outright mutual hostility from the start? Would they even have a language in common? The words formed in the air like crystals in a dish.

'If you can't get up under your own power,' Cosimo said, 'you don't deserve to be here.'

'It's not how you get uphill that counts, it's how you get down again,' Callahan retorted. 'Let's shred, dude.'

He shot down the mountainside, no poles, arcs of snow pluming up from his skis like feathers. Cosimo took off after him and caught him in an instant. Then they were zigzagging down, weaving in and out of one another's slipstreams like the Aspen As. I went hooning straight through the middle of them, clinging to the hypotenuse, the ideal and fastest line. Callahan and Cosimo pulled level, one on either side of me. Now we were all gliding in parallel tramlines and Cosimo and Callahan eyed each other with respect. We sprang over camels and crevasses, we outsmarted the hazards of mousetraps and dogsheads, we bisected forests and ravines, we went past Steve Lee and the Bells and Girardelli and Tomba and Andrea Cova.

Now there was no one else but us. We had exchanged our skis for snowboards and we were carving across the face, poised on our single edge, drawing voluptuous triple sine curves in the snow. We pressed down hard and the compacted hexagons turned to a river beneath our boards and the river turned into a sea and the water was warm and blue and we were in the thunderous tube. We trimmed to hold fast to our line, neither sliding up and over the falls nor down and into the pit. As the spit blew us out through the snake's eye it seemed to me that the three of us had become one and the one was all three. On the golden beach in the shade of a palm tree Heather was waving at me and our son was building castles in the sand. I lay down while the benevolent wave cradled me towards the shore and high above I could see Elja, hovering like a helicopter, beaming down from the astral plane. Then the sky darkened and an avalanche out of nowhere hit me and I was rolled round for ever under a million tons of snow and rocks and stones and trees.

'I heard someone at the Press Centre laughing about some English guy puking his guts up in his room – I knew it had to be you.' It sounded like Callahan. He thrust a yard-long lens in my face and pulled the trigger. It was Callahan.

'I thought you were in the Gulf,' I groaned.

'I've been on the Highway of Death. The worst traffic jam I ever saw.'

Now my eyes were starting to focus again I could see he was wearing a stretch neoprene shirt emblazoned with the slogans: 'THE POWDER AND THE GLORY' and 'MAKE MADNESS A WAY OF LIFE'.

Like Montgomery, Callahan dreamed of snow in the desert. 'There were some fast slopes. When the sun was straight overhead the sand was almost white. It swirled up in your face like fine powder. In a jeep you could do some neat linked turns and schuss at fifty mph.'

Callahan described a photograph he'd taken of a burned-out truck with two soldiers incinerated where they sat in the front seats, skeletons staring out of where the windscreen used to be, with sand blowing through their bones, and piled up behind, an endless convoy of wreckage, a mutilated, twisted, frazzled bomb sculpture. It still wasn't the Perfect Picture: he'd thought of shooting the belly of a bomber at the instant its bay doors open and release its load. But he wasn't ready for posthumous fame yet. Fuck art.

'I've had the big bad dark thing up to here. God, it's good to be cold again. You coming to Lake Louise? Jesus, you're not going to miss that too?'

Epilogue

It was summer. Patrick Lang was working as a producer for CBS on the Tour de France; I bumped into him by the finish line in Le Havre. 'Hello, Mr Martin,' he said. While the cyclists were grinding along tarmac several hours every day for a month, the downhill skiers, when you added it all up, raced for less than thirty minutes a year. On the other hand, if you joined together all the trips they had made up and down mountains they would reach to the moon.

Now they were sliding down a glacier somewhere in the southern hemisphere, in Argentina or Australia or New Zealand, in search of the endless winter, training for the season to come. Franz Heinzer, after winning the second event at Lake Louise, was the 1991 Downhill Champion, with Atle Skaardal, who had won the first, runner-up. Marc Girardelli won the slalom and the overall World Cup title, leaving Alberto Tomba with the consolation prize of the giant slalom. George was on the trail of Steve Lee up at Falls Creek in the Snowy Mountains.

Cosimo was back in Cambridge and Callahan was in Hawaii. For all my efforts to arrange a meeting, they never met up, except in my mind, where they were roped together for all time.

Elja had gone in for rebirthing.

In August Callahan got me a job as official British

victim in the Hawaiian International Ocean Challenge at Waikiki, where lifeguards from the four corners of the earth would be battling it out to rescue me. 'The water's a constant 82 degrees,' his fax read. 'Do you think you can handle that?' I was saved by a man named Melvyn Pu'u whose last name meant mountain. His favourite training routine consisted of picking up an eighty-pound rock and running along the seabed with it until his lungs burst.

Callahan shot a whole roll of Melvyn Pu'u taking an improvised shower under a hosepipe. Then he went off to play the part of a small-time crook and heartthrob in a Japanese cops and robbers film.

It was around the same time that Pierre Tardivel was climbing Everest, following Hillary up the Col Sud. He knew that was the easy route, he said, 'but it was still an interesting itinerary.' He invited me along too, as if it were a Sunday picnic. It was six days march from Kathmandu. According to the averages, Pierre's ten-strong team and ten sherpas had only a one-in-four chance of making it to the top. His wife Kathy waited at base camp for a month. Sometimes she would check on his progress up the face through a telescope, but it made her nervous. In reality, Pierre was pushing everyone hard, frequently taking over the lead position in his impatience to get to the summit. But from that distance it looked like a hesitant ascent: for every three steps up he made two steps down again. The idea of acclimatization was to thin out the red corpuscles that threatened to freeze and block the veins, causing frostbite. But Pierre was cold all the way up from Camp Two. He didn't feel bad, and eventually he didn't feel anything. In the teeth of 60 mph winds, they made it to Camp

Four at 8000 metres, 800 metres short of the summit, from where Miura had begun his spiralling fall, and sat it out for the night.

By daybreak both Pierre's feet had turned blue-black. He would go down to the camp below for a few days to get medical help, and then come back up. This time he had to come down without his skis. But he didn't go up again: it was stay down or lose his right foot. It took months for the toenails to grow back. Pierre made one error: his boots, the ones he had had made specially with the velcro fastenings, were too tight and not warm enough. It was impossible to test them for Everest at minus 40 or 50 anywhere other than on Everest.

Next time he would take bigger, warmer boots and he would let others make the pace. He left a pair of Jeannot Liard's Vertical Extremes, a lump of Bertrand's *haute montagne* wax, and a bottle of oxygen at Kathmandu: he would be back the next summer. And after Everest? There were a dozen summits over 8000 metres in the Himalayas, all of them unskied. K2, Kanchenjunga, Annapurna, still beckoned.

Michael Willis was my Jeannot Liard. But while Dynastar manufactured a million skis a year, he was lucky to make one surfboard a week. Waves were more important than work. On the day I went to see him – my last in Hawaii – he was shaping in his back garden, wearing a surgeon's mask over his nose as protection against the dust. Two winters before he had promised me the perfect board, but he'd never made it. It wasn't that he was bluffing or lazy, it was just that it was hard in reality to come up with the kind of perfection he had in mind. 'This is destiny,' he said. 'I'm working on your board right now. It's perfect.' As we were parting I told him I was writing a book about mountains. 'This was meant to be,' he said.

It was a part of the North Shore I'd never been to before, up towards Kaena Point, where in winter fifty-foot waves pounded the reef. There was no tarmac road between the North Shore and the West Side, only a rough dirt track, rutted and pot-holed. We bumped and weaved along it for a mile or so. There were no other cars, nothing but the ocean on one side and the hills on the other.

'You know Manimi fish?' Michael said.

'No.'

'When you see them swimming together, it's like they've all got one brain – they don't signal or anything, but when one turns, they all turn.'

Michael's mountain was only two or three thousand feet high. At the top was an astronomical observatory. From the bottom it looked like a gentle climb.

'What do you call it?' I asked.

'I call it a Helluvalottawork.' That was the only name Michael gave it, it had no other.

I had on shorts and thongs for the beach. 'Do you think I'm wearing the right gear for this climb?'

'Andy, you're overdressed.' Michael was barefoot.

We waded through the bush at the bottom of the hill and began to climb upwards with the midday sun blowtorching our backs. I soon realized this mountain was more difficult than I was counting on. It was an extinct volcano whose sides were composed of chunks of dried-up lava, black boulders with deep crevices between. It was like stepping stones across a river where the torrent threatens to carry you off and fling you over the falls. Michael bounded from one to the other with the instinctive agility of a mountain goat, barely pausing to look down. I scrabbled for footholds and every time I looked up he was a long way off and gaining.

'Think of it as a flight of stairs,' he said helpfully. He was sitting amid some rocks halfway up.

'I call this the King's Throne.' There was a flat horizontal seat and a perpendicular backrest. 'Look, there's even a spot for the King to put his beer.' Michael placed an imaginary mug on a small, round ledge.

He stood up and invited me to rest on the King's Throne. 'There's a time to go fast and a time to go slow.'

Clambering up, I had been cursing Michael and wishing I'd gone up Everest with Pierre Tardivel after all. It was from such modest heights overlooking the Irish Sea that Arnold Lunn had fallen and smashed his leg. But now all the anxiety seemed to seep out of me into the rocks and I felt as light as air. I looked out on the hill dropping away below me and far away the sun-streaked sea and the blue-rinsed sky and further still, across the channel, I could make out the neighbouring island of Kauai rising up out of the water. Never before had I seen so clearly that Hawaii was nothing but a chain of mountains peering up out of the Pacific like periscopes. All islands were mountains, all continents were. Where the waves broke was the beginning of the foothills. Dante's Purgatorio, I remembered, was not just a mountain with terraces connected by stairways in the rock, but an island, the only land in the southern hemisphere, at the antipodes to Jerusalem.

I climbed up higher and found Michael lying with his face to the sun and a blade of grass between his lips. 'You see those rocks,' he said, not opening his eyes, 'they're so crumbly you could slip here and fall all the way down and never stop.' The higher you went the smaller the rocks were, until there was only dust left at the top. Michael sounded pleased at the prospect of falling, as if it were an experience to be looked forward to and savoured.

'Get out your bow and arrow,' Michael said. There were wild boar in the forest on the far side of the ridge. We were at the top of the hill, in the domed shadow of the observatory, but we hadn't finished yet. Eagle Rock was a promontory that projected out over the abyss and it was the highest point. Michael wanted us to stand on it and for me to carve my name in the stone.

We picked our way along the thin path at the top like tightrope walkers. A squally wind gusted in our faces as if to blow us off and a heavy rain began to fall. We sheltered in the lee of Eagle Rock. 'You're going to have to save up the top for next time,' Michael said. 'Here's my knife. Carve your name anyway. Right here next to mine.'

Something made me think of the Australian aboriginal mythology of the dreamtime. 'According to their idea, mountains were poems before they were mountains and they had to be sung into existence.'

'It's possible,' Michael said. 'I don't know. It's like Mount Fuji. Climbing up one side, you could be on the moon. Coming down the other, it's green, like a park. Neither side is the whole truth.'

Michael gazed out over the open ocean. 'Can't you see the winter coming from up here?' Two days before, the North Shore had seen what everyone called, even in August, 'the first signs of winter': a solid overhead swell which rolled in suddenly and then as quickly disappeared, like an augury. 'In winter, the waves at the Point are the size of mountains. They're as hard and heavy as mountains.'

The rain turned the red dust to mud and I slid and slithered in my thongs until a strap came loose. This was as far off-piste as it was possible to go. I felt for a moment that the whole winter had been an illusion and that midnight had struck and my skis had turned back into a pumpkin.

Michael took the shoe and rammed the rubber anchor back in its slot and scrubbed the deck dry with a handful of grass.

'Won't going down be even harder?' I said.

'It's even easier – gravity takes you down, doesn't it?' Michael replied.

He took off and ran down to meet the ocean. Halfway down the slope I found a scrawled note he had left me under a stone:

ANDY
TURN HERE

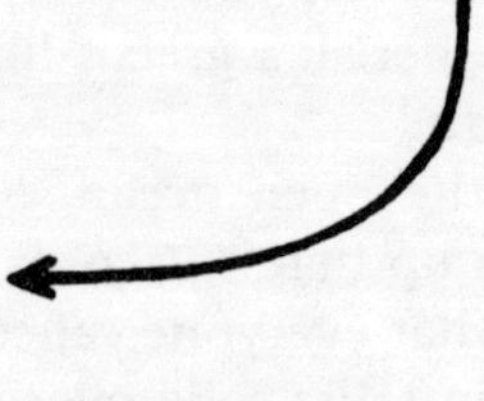